GASLIGHTING

Learn How to Definitevely Break the Cycle of
Emotional

(How to Avoid the Gaslight Effect and Heal From
Emotional Abuse)

William Simpso

Published By Oliver Leish

William Simpson

All Rights Reserved

Gaslighting: Learn How to Definitevely Break the Cycle of Emotional (How to Avoid the Gaslight Effect and Heal From Emotional Abuse)

ISBN 978-1-77485-246-0

Legal & Disclaimer

The information contained in this book is not designed to replace or take the place of any form of medicine or professional medical advice. The information in this book has been provided for educational and entertainment purposes only.

The information contained in this book has been compiled from sources deemed reliable, and it is accurate to the best of the Author's knowledge; however, the Author cannot guarantee its accuracy and validity and cannot be held liable for any errors or omissions. Changes are periodically made to this book. You must consult your doctor or get professional medical advice before using any of the suggested remedies, techniques, or information in this book.

TABLE OF CONTENTS

Introduction

I'll teach you everything you must be aware of about gaslighting. It may seem like you've learned everything you need to know about this method of manipulation However, this book is not like other books out on the market that you've read.

However, when you read the numerous books available in the marketplace about gaslighting, and how narcissists utilize this method to abuse and harm the person they are in a relationship however, there's not enough details about the particular strategies. You may only go through a chapter at the very least and a blurb at best. The details about gaslighting as a manipulative, narcissistic technique is extremely insufficient in numerous books, and could even be lacking. There's a lot more to know about this!

You've taken a extremely smart choice by opting to buy a version of the book. I'm confident that you'll find it modern, useful, and practical. It's not worth to discuss the various ways that you could be gaslit by a

Narcissist, without providing concrete instances of the gaslighting in the real world, as well as ways to tackle the issue. Gaslighting is a extremely harmful technique that has a wide-ranging impact in the event that one fails to see the signs or take steps to safeguard themselves. To tackle gaslighting as well as narcissistsone must be able to do a more than not recognizing well-known facts.

Are there a person who is a narcissist in your life who make your day life miserable? Would you like to end their snarky ways, and take back control of your life for once forever? You have the right to live your most fulfilling life. This includes in addition to that it is to not allow people or situations that are causing you to lose your joy or peace. The dangers of toxic people are real and so are the issues they cause. It's not easy to stay clear of them or be willing to sacrifice for them until they drain the vitality out of one. It's about knowing how to handle them in the manner in a manner that they receive the message that you are certainly not a victim. You won't allow you to be snubbed by.

The majority of books dump information onto you. This book is distinct. At the end of this book, you'll be able to handle gaslighting to ensure that you remain sane and dignified as well as your sanity intact.

Chapter 1: What Exploitation Is - And What It Actually Feels Like

How do you know if you're being tricked? What are the signs that someone is tampering with your thoughts and feelings in the hope of exploitation to gain the sake of their selfish and unsavory gain?

Sometimes you're able to almost believe that the person you're dealing with is to nothing. There's a unsettling feeling in the background that something's not there. It's as if nothing is like it is each time you talk to the person. You'd like you to offer them the benefit belief, however you cannot. It's hard to tell whether you're the crazy person in this situation. Let's take a look at all the crazy thoughts that you've got floating around in your head as a un-lovable collection of fish!

If you're being controlled psychologically it's as if your thoughts are being directed towards making the wrong decisions and conclusions. It's like you're feeling that your feelings are being used to gain advantage and you're not able to figure out the reason and how it's happening. You feel like you're losing control. It's not from a position of authority in a manipulative relationship.

Aren't We Always Being Manipulated?

It's simple to answer this question. It seems like there's a very thin line that separates benign social influence as well as malignant manipulative behavior. It's not so thin. It's not uncommon to see people socially influence each other. It's a part of connecting with each other in a healthy manner. How can you tell the difference between this kind of healthy interaction and manipulative behavior? If you're being targeted you feel like the person who is manipulating you is doing it for their own gain and at your expense. They have a plan and you feel it when they twist and turn your body to achieve what they would like. However, they're so smooth at their craft, you start to doubt your intuition regarding what's happening

-and that's just one of the purposes for the manipulator.

How to Find Out if You're A Victim of Manipulation

We'll go through a set of questions that you must ask yourself in the hope of determining whether you're being the victim of psychological or emotional manipulative behavior. Bring to mind those friendships or relationships that make you wonder what the intentions of the other person are while you consider these questions.

I'm trying to make it clear that these questions aren't necessarily the final word in figuring out the possibility of being a victim. But they will reveal the areas in the course of your daily life. you've been overtly or covertly controlled. Keep in the mind that just because you are aware of the things mentioned here isn't a guarantee that you suggest that you're being controlled. Sometimes, it's a simple scenario in which your person is exhibiting a few undesirable characteristics and that's all there is to it. It's crucial to know when you're being taken advantage of and depleted by the manipulative personalist in your personal life.

Questions

1. Do you feel that you're not on the same level with the other person? Perhaps you've observed that every when you meet them your feelings are like a fish that has gone under the water. It's almost as if where the conversation is taking place it's like you're in their space and not mine; not somewhere neutral , where you feel that you are on the same level of respect. You may have noticed every interaction you have takes place in a way that is not only where they'd like it to but whenever they wish it to. There's no thought given to what's most ideal for you. It feels as though you're always in their home, or their office, or their insert-random-place-here. It's not as if that you're in a familiar physical or mentally when you communicate with them.

2. Do you notice that when you meet, you must first speak? Perhaps you've observed that whenever you get together, you're always the first to speak. Inevitably, you feel vulnerable. You're feeling as if, because you've had to first speak and then be questioned for weaknesses that could be used to gain advantage. It's like they're trying to figure out what drives you in order to strike you in the areas that hurt. This is a fantastic method to make the sale, yet it can have negative consequences when your partner who is narcissistic employs it against you.

3. If you have a conversation with them Do you find yourself feeling that they will always find a way to twist or bend the truth? They can tell a falsehood and you're puzzled because you're not certain what prompted them to lie. They offer excuses, and even though you think these are a bunch of excuses but you don't want to be a rude bully by holding those responsible for their behavior. You're trying to get things working However, they decide to blame you even though an impartial third

party, such as the United Nations, and everyone's grandmother would confirm their assertion that the issue was not their fault, but yours. They make statements that sound like truth, however the facts and your gut make you believe there's a lie. It's their own interpretation of what happened. You've noticed that they reveal information in the event that they believe they can benefit from it as well, and they've got a habit of withholding important details from you. Every when they talk to you or speak, they're either denying the facts to make you feel like an outrageously dramatic nut-job who has made Mount Rushmore out of a pebble. When they're not understating facts they're exaggerating them making you feel like the child from Frankenstein or Loch Ness Monster! Loch Ness Monster!

4. Do they burden you with their intelligence and intelligence? You might have observed that you find yourself feeling like a fool when you talk with them. They'll scold you with their intellect while they spit out all the statistics and

facts on you , so they can sway you , since you're only aware of so much. It's like they've got all the information and facts, you are forced other than to follow the agenda they're trying to push. Sometimes, it's to achieve a particular goal. Sometimes, they simply want to dominate you.

5. If you speak do they have a habit of constantly shouting and expressing negativity? Some manipulators make use of their voice to intimidate others in order to obtain what they desire. If you're constantly prone to feel inadequate, small and withdrawn because of their rage there's a good chance it's an incident. In addition to getting increasingly louder, but they can become extremely dramatic with their bodies and also. You think that the only way to stop this is to surrender in. They are also not afraid of being a part of the group which makes you feel shamed and embarrassed. People won't shout at you. They'll be so clear about their pain or disappointment that you're not willing to give in to their demands which makes you

feel guilty about standing and speaking up. It's a more subtle type of manipulative tactics, with the ultimate aim of forcing you to accept what they want.

6. Are you always surprised(in a bad way) and off balance with someone? Surprises can be pleasant. But they can also be very unpleasant. You might have noticed that the person you're talking to is a great fan of unpleasant kind of surprise. They will throw a "surprise" on you and you are off balance instantly, as your brain is trying to comprehend things. Your emotions are exactly as the manipulator is looking for. These surprises come your way and you are feeling like you're unable to stop these surprises. You don't have any plans to to deal these surprises.

7. Does this person constantly give you with ultimatums? You are under a significant pressure to do or say something that you wouldn't normally do, because they've handed you a order: take this action, or else you'll be forced to comply with that. It's clear to you that there are

other choices however, they've given you only A or. There aren't any other letters in the alphabet they are aware of! You are under pressure to take action and act and give in to whatever they want from you.

8. Do they have a habit of laughing in your face? You may have noticed this manipulative person is fond of be funny about you. They make this happen whenever there are people in your vicinity, which makes you feel stupid or incompetent. Sometimes they'll do this even in the case of just two of you to make you feel as if that you're making a thing into a major deal. Never think about whether it's actually a significant issue. No matter what the reason the jokes they tell are intended in order to create a feeling of less than. You feel unsecure. You feel sluggish even though they're smiling. This is the way to go. The ultimate goal would be being the best dogpsychologically speaking.

9. Do they judge and criticize your every whim? True manipulators does this, and

don't bother to give you constructive feedback or suggestions on ways to improve at what they're criticizing you for. It's clear that they don't care about helping you become more effective. In the event that they are, you'll find yourself feeling "less than" around them. It's like you're not adequate enough. They criticize, nitpick and criticize, but all with a soft tone of tone as well as a smile. They might even put in a tender, loving touch to add a little sweetness. But, you're always feeling as if you're being mocked. You are aware that your thoughts and ideas are disregarded. You're being snubbed into obscurity. You think you're giving a 100%, but regardless of the effort you put into it and how better at it you become you'll always appear less than desirable in their eye.

10. Do they provide you with a silence until you say what they'd like to say? They repress you and you are left incapable of doing anything about the situation. Every attempt to communicate by you are ignored which makes you feel less

helpless. The manipulator is aware of this. You feel as if you're waiting in limbo, but for what reason? It's hard to say. The longer they hold you back for them to finish, the more uncomfortable, uncertain, and uncertain of your decision. They'll keep pushing when they have to, but they'll not speak up they believe they've punished you enough or until you give in and let them have the things they need.

11. Have you observed that this person is in the practice of not knowing? They're known to play dumb of what your wants and requirements are, and forget that you've spoken to them in 500 or 2,500, 6.000 different ways and numerous times! You're frustrated with this, and do not know what else to do other than to put it down and shut up.

12. Do your conversations with the person result in you feeling guilty? There are a myriad of ways that this could happen. The manipulator is skilled in shifting blame in this kind of a way that if unaware, you are prone to taking it upon yourself. You

begin to feel guilty because of things that have no connection to your own actions. Your weaknesses and weaknesses are used to shamelessly by the manipulator, so that you are forced to follow their instructions.

13. Does this person possess a ability to play the victim, even though they're not? You might have noticed that they love being the dog that has been injured. This is a perfect excuse to hide their savage behaviour. If they are suffering from health issues you can be sure they'll use them to their advantage. If they don't have health issues they'll just create them. It's like every word that comes out of their mouths, each move they make is carefully designed to draw you in and making you feel sorry for them or inspire you to help them. You've probably observed you've noticed in all stories, they're or are the weak, unprotected one, or self-sacrificing heroes. All of this is to make you do something from the kindness of your heart or to make use of that moral sense obligation.

If you've answered "yes" to a majority or all of them, it's clear that you're dealing with. A manipulator. A thought-bender, who can fill your mind with what they like. A mood-bender, making you feel whatever is going to work with them in the final.

If you think you could have been in a affair with a person who is a narcissist, you shouldn't remain in a solitary position and not do anything! Get professional help right away and consult a certified psychiatrist, or a expert in the mental health field to get the right advice for your particular situation.

Chapter 2: Accepting The Ins And Outs Of Gaslighting

It was 1944 when a film titled Gaslight was released, which revolutionized the way people think of manipulation, and it's incredible impact. The film tells the story of a husband who manipulates his wife their life in such a way that she believes that she has gone insane.

In this film also, the wife, Paula is completely obsessed with the attraction of Gregory who charms and woos her. After a intense relationship, they tie the knot but then the heartbreak starts. Gregory begins to reveal his true personality in such a subtle way that Paula begins to think everything is fine with her husband, and that she's going insane.

In the film, the husband in the film dimmed the gas light in the home and claimed that his wife believed that the lights were dim. The force of his argument and manipulation were so strong that the unfortunate woman starts to believe that she's gone insane. The term gaslighting was used to refer to such devious and sinister manipulative techniques to intentionally divert people from their actual life and experiences.

The film itself is an adaptation of a 1938 play with the same title. The main goal of the husband who was a villain was to cause his wife's insanity to lock her up in a mentally ill institution to take her inheritance.

Gaslighting is a term employed by psychologists to refer to the methods employed by people suffering from a mental disorder in order to influence and control the lives of others who are either people as individuals, and/or a group of individuals. They are so effective and deep that the people who are controlled tend to doubt every aspect in their lives, their actual thoughts and perceptions, and experiences of their experiences. If you can experience such a maniacal hold on your personal life there's no doubt the safety of your family and mental health are in danger.

In this moment, it is crucial to distinguish the gaslighting tactics from those that are used by many to upset and cause annoyance to those who are around them. Gaslighting techniques are characterized by a negative aspect that the an innocuous, yet annoying actions of certain individuals don't possess. It is crucial to discern the difference between these two to ensure that you don't end in judging anyone you meet with incorrectly.

However, you should be sure that the practice of gaslighting poses a serious problem and you should be able to spot such behaviors and stay as far from people who are prone to this kind of behavior as you can. The truth is being able to take your reality from you could be extremely risky, and if it is not handled with care, it could be disastrous for you and your family members.

The challenge in gaslighting is that the behaviors may start as something small and unimportant. For instance, the manipulator may rectify a small aspect in a story or event you're narrating. Naturally, the reason for their corrections make sense, and you take it with full confidence. Then, the 'past victory is the main focus and it keeps rearing it's ugly face in all interactions with the person who is concerned And before you know it, you are the victim of his or her plight, completely losing touch with reality and your life.

If you are careful, you'll be pressured to the degree that making simple choices may become complicated for you. Motivated by self-doubt seeds that are sown by the gaslighter you may find yourself second-guessing each decision that you take. In the end the victim will think that they can't make any choice and is dependent on every aspect of the manipulator.

In addition, the person who is at fault will gradually convince you that the behaviour is in fact your blame. If you are able to apologize for your conduct and the more greedier the person's ego grows and they will demand an ever-increasing amount of apology and supplicating behavior from you.

The aggressor is so sucked into the gaslighting mindset that it becomes extremely difficult to seek assistance from other people in the worry that they might go against you. If you are totally and irrevocably in the hands of the person who is in control, the aggressor is able to take you out and search for new 'conquests.'

History of Gaslighting

Although the term "gaslighting" was first introduced in the 1940s, the idea of manipulative behaviour to control individuals and altering their imagined realities has been an integral in the history of mankind for a long period of. The victims were merely diagnosed as having this disorder. They left to rot in a insane asylum or in another institution isolated, depressed and totally ignored.

Do you remember the story of "The Emperor's Clothes What transpired there? Did the salesman's cleverness cause all the people who looked at him into believing that the Emperor was clad in the most exquisite of clothes but, in reality, he was naked? A child, innocent of guilt helped save the day for those who believed that were unable to discern the clothes worn by their Emperor, it was their fault.

In 1981 the psychology professor Edward Weinshel wrote an article entitled "Some Clinical Consequences of Introjection: Gaslighting," in which he described the concept in the following manner. The manipulator "externalizes" and projecting the thought or image and the victim then is able to internalize and absorb the information into their mental psyche without question. The victim takes in all the flaws of the manipulator, their mistakes, and the irrationality in these relationships.

Why Does Gaslighting Happen?

Gaslighting is about controlling. This desire for dominance or control could result from personality disorders such as Narcissism, social issues and unresolved childhood trauma or any other cause.

Gaslighting is typically seen as a result of people being who are involved in power dynamics in which one person is always in the position of having more power than another person or persons in the relationship. The victim of the gaslighting techniques usually falls located on a lower in the hierarchy than the manipulator, and is also afraid of losing the things in their relationship. The victim in the relationship that is manipulative most likely to become a codependent member in that relationship.

For instance, in a romantic relationship it is possible that the wife feels the need to live with the manipulative behavior of her partner because she wants to participate in the relationship and/or wants the other benefits it can bring. People like this are prepared to shift their perspective to reflect those of their manipulative partner to prevent conflicts and allow things to flow easily.

However the manipulator will continue to behave like a 'target' because they are afraid of being perceived as being less significant or more important than they want to be. Another crucial aspect on the part of the gaslighter person might not even realize that they are acting in ways that might be harmful or detrimental to the target. They may be engaging in gaslighting techniques due to the fact that they were raised as such.

Where Does Gaslighting Happen?

Gaslighting can occur and be experienced by anyone and. As an example, you might find yourself a victim of these tactics from your partner, spouse or coworker, or perhaps a parent. Gaslighting techniques aren't limited to the professional or personal area.

Gaslighting tactics are employed in public life, and affect the entire population. There are many instances in which it is clear to observe the gaslighting tactics employed utilized by the president Donald Trump and his administration. Many experts agree that politics is a discipline where lying is considered as a typical way of life. But the president Trump has taken his stance a little too far.

In the first few days of his administration the president Trump and his staff members is believed to have deceived the American public in such a way that it lent a hint of arrogance, and total disregard for the wisdom of the American citizens. It was as if worried officials were trying to lure the people of all ages by telling them to get up and protest against the infidels if they could. This was a obvious sign of narcissism personality disorder.

In one instance, they made up about the size of the crowd during the Presidential swearing-in. It was evident that the pictures from the swearing-in ceremony were altered to look similar to the one that is currently in place. It was that it was simple to recognize this falsehood that for some this was a warning to the media that was likely to be criticized by Americans for having such lies on their sites and in their publications.

On a individual level these techniques are employed by manipulative individuals who wish to influence the family life of their loved ones. Consider a emotionally and physically destructive spouse who causes havoc on the other spouse or kids in their family and you will be able to quickly spot gaslighting behaviour.

Where is Gaslighting Typically Seen?

Gaslighting in general is not restricted to just one region of the globe. Anywhere power dynamic is in the game and the desire and need to exert control over individuals and resources is present the gaslighting behaviour is evident. Numerous studies show that this type of unsafe and unattractive behavior is not just seen in interpersonal relationships but also in work and even in public life in the way that politicians and their entourage interact with everyday people in the street.

MHR is an HR service provider has performed a poll in the UK that revealed shocking figures. The survey was completed by over 3000 participants. survey which revealed that 58% the people claimed to have encountered what they thought was gas-lighting in their workplace. Around 30% of respondents said that they didn't experience this behaviour, while 12 percent said that they did not know! The alarming results of this survey demonstrate how widespread gazlighting has become in Britain. UK. Examples of gaslighting practices in the workplace are:

Crediting your work

You, your conduct or dress in the presence of colleagues

Making deadlines that are unrealistic and unreasonable

The deliberate withholding of information is vital to the achievement of a project you're working on

Many of the factors that are mentioned above appear to be minor however they add up to a quite a lot in the future. Furthermore, in contrast to the behavior of bullying that is easily detectable, gaslighting behavior is subtle and intended to gradually, but slowly, cast doubt on your abilities and the value of your company. They aren't discovered until the damage has been done to the target's psychological health.

A different report from the United States states says that 3 out of 4 citizens in the US aren't conscious of the concept, and this apathy is in spite of the prevalence of gaslighting in both the entertainment as well as media industries, where power-playing dynamics are among the most powerful.

Seventy percent of respondents said they'd been aware of the term, but were unsure of its significance. The research revealed that around a third of females had described their partner as 'crazy or insane' in a very serious manner. A quarter of males also used these words to describe their loved ones.

Thus, the gaslighting practice isn't restricted to a particular region or industry It can be observed in various countries, cultures and even industries.

Common Gaslighting Situations

Here are some scenarios of gaslighting that can help you figure out whether and how you might be being gaslighted by a variety of culprits.

In a family environment, Alice's father Andrew is a angry and bitter man, who has carried a large amount of negative emotions in his early years. Andrew's power play is the most apparent with Alice due to her dependence on Andrew for a many things. The mother of Alice is main breadwinner in the family, and spends the majority of her time working.

Alice had spent a much more times with her dad than she did her mother, and unknowingly pushed herself into a codependency relationship with Andrew. She was extremely attuned to Andrew's mood changes and was constantly anxious that an act or behaviour of hers could trigger a depression in her father.

If the father of Alice was in a sad state of mind, her father would shout out at Alice with a sarcastic "You're useless," "I am not sure why you were born and often using foul language , too. If Alice tried to argue with him then he would smile it off and then ask "Why are you being so sensitive?

Alice was so used to the situation within her own home. She didn't consider it necessary to talk to her mother who was working too much to be able to spend time with her daughter. Alice was totally in the hands of her father and took it as a natural. Alice thought that the father was aiding her in self-improvement and she believed there was nothing wrong with him.

Another scenario that is common is when children of adulthood play with their parents' old age. Here's a example of a situation that is likely to be found in several homes.

In a romance - in the eyes of many people, Julie's lifestyle could be viewed as perfect. For more than five years, she was married with her initial love, who has since become a devoted husband financially stable (her partner, John, is an investment banker who makes in the money) and blessed with two gorgeous children, Julie could appear as if there is a lot of joy in the world. But she's aware of the struggle she's facing. Prior to her marriage, Julie was an artist with a lot of talent.

When she was married, John did his best to keep his wife from attempting to improve her abilities and create a mark for herself in the world of art. He would always criticize the work she did and made her believe that it was inadequate. Every time she attempted to create anything, the man would comment"A poor artist like you're not going to be able to survive in the art world , which is brimming with talented artists. Your work isn't going to stand the work of theirs. Do not waste your time or dollars on this. Instead, concentrate on taking care of your family.'

He would also mention a unpleasant experience she was a victim of during her first days of art. She had designed a painting and sought to hear by a well-known artist, who happened to be a close partner to her husband's. The man had stated that her abilities were far below that of an average artist and she shouldn't even bother taking the next step. Julie's husband was always quick to mention that statement and use it to make her believe she was suited to do nothing but take charge of the family.

Julie's husband used the one negative event and feedback to remind her of her insignificance constantly, and repeatedly and habitual behavior led to the enslavement of the woman to his husband for life. While she's living in a comfortable lifestyle, she is aware the fact that she is empty. She is determined to free herself from her husband's manipulations however, he is using their children to increase his control over her.

In a work environment - Jolly was a salesperson in a large showroom for cosmetics. After five years of working she was awarded a advancement that did not just mean she earned a more lucrative salary but also provided opportunities for career advancement. Jolly was thrilled after her promotion and began working under their new supervisor, Penny.

At first, Jolly found Penny helpful and sweet. Gradually, Penny started passing on minor tasks to Jolly and she did the work without complaint. But, it didn't slow down or, in fact, increased enough that she didn't have the time or energy to study any new skills at work. She was being able to complete every task given by her boss, which kept her arms distance and discouraged interaction in all forms, except for assigning tasks.

A departmental meeting was held the other day and Jolly was present. Penny addressed the others and asked"Meet Jolly who has been here for over three months and is still trying to master the ropes of the department she joined. I'm hoping that she can catch up soon , or else we'll be forced to deport her after her demotion.' Jolly turned red in embarrassment and shame over the open and sudden insult by her boss. She realized that she had been a victim of gaslighting techniques!

Emotional Hot Spots are targeted

Anyone could be a victim to gaslighting techniques due to the subtleties involved in the method. Few people are able to recognize the distinction between gaslighting and just plain irritating behaviour. The majority of people typically classify the gaslighting behavior as a minor nuisance and choose to overlook it. But, there are certain categories of people who are easily to gaslight. There are a few of them:

People who are insecure are the most vulnerable people. Gaslighters generally target people who have substantial inferiority complexes. Women and men who are unsecure about themselves are prime to target because they're in a vulnerable state.

Furthermore, those who are insecure constantly seek positive reinforcement from others This is precisely what they want from gaslighters in the beginning stages of any relationship. Gaslighting strategies begin with giving praise, even but not always and also praising victims at first, but once they're trapped by the tactics, the real colors of the gaslighters will come to the forefront.

However, it's the right time to remind everyone that gaslighters are so skilled in their work that even the smartest and most rational people could be targeted by them. So, it is sensible to be aware of gaslighting and its many negative consequences, and to be aware of those who use them.

Chapter 3: Gaslighting In Dealings

A lot of us struggle with anxiety, depression, and crippling self-doubt. We don't believe that our feelings are legitimate and we've been raised in the context of homes where we've learned that thoughts and emotions aren't worth much and therefore we do not bother to analyze our own minds and ask questions that could aid in identifying gaslighting behavior.

In order to recognize the gaslighting behaviours You must be capable of loving yourself and explore your inner self. You must be someone who isn't shy about expressing yourself , and someone who is proficient in creating limits. You must be someone who doesn't struggle with codependency. If you're a highly empathic and compassionate person you'll be a major target for gaslighting because you'll always be trying to help others and keep trying to figure out how other people behave.

If you are accused of doing something you're not guilty of, such as lying, you should attempt to convince the person in question that you're not lying. You will, in the same way show them that you cherish them. You must learn about gaslighting and how to recognize gaslighting. When you're gaslighted, you do not really think there's something wrong with you, which is why you remain in an unreliable relationship. This is the kind of thing that psychopaths and narcissists frequently do. It's a strategy they employ to manipulate their victims. They do this because they want their people they are targeting to hide the truth about them. Even if they're cheating with you, they would rather not lose you since you are their main source of income, so they'll continue to lie to you about their cheating.

If you've informed a someone who is a narcissist that you're in a relationship by the person you kissed in the pub, they will inform you that you didn't tell them about you were kissing the person in the pub. They'll make up scenarios to justify what really occurred, but they'll never acknowledge the truth. They will continue to attack you and claim that nobody thinks the way you do, or If you were not vulnerable, then you shouldn't have made that statement. He'll claim that he was communicating with them. They'll tell you that you're so unsure and that every single guy or woman you've had a relationship with has been cheating on you. So now that you have seen me talk about a girl, you think I'm cheating you. Then you'll think twice, particularly when you have a traumatized background.

If you're dealing somebody who is great at gaslighting you'll be the one who will end in apologizing to them for being gaslighted. The person you apologize to will state for your pity that you have ever accused him of kissing the girl, or sorry that you caused him to feel offended. Then, the gaslighter might respond with something similar to, "oh, I can't believe you're accusing me of doing something similar to this. You've hurt me in a lot of ways by accusing me of doing such a act".

Now you're not just in denial and making you question what you've stated, but they want you to feel guilty about your words and manipulate your feelings even more.

You must be aware of that. If you're in a relationship which makes you feel like you're insane or a one that makes it feels like you're in a boxing fight with someone you're meant to be your love If you feel like this, then you're in a romantic relationship that is gaslighted.

If you feel that you're in a unkind relationship in which your significant other is likely to make you feel guilty for speaking to a topic or to make you feel guilty for not making them feel happy, or punish you for suggesting they're people who lie or lying, then it is possible that you are in a unsatisfied relationship. If you're in a relationship with someone who has shown a negative attitude towards them the relationship, it's time to review the relationship. If you're in a relationship that makes you feel crazed and makes you question your reality this means you're in a unsatisfied relationship.

No matter how clever and intelligent you believe you are, anyone who excels at gaslighting could fool you. One thing a psychopath and a narcissist a psychopath can do is impress you and get you to feel safe with them. They're extremely attractive. They are doing this because they would like you to be more open. They're trying to reveal your flaws. When you begin to feel at ease, you'll begin sharing with them how you feel , and they'll begin collecting data and writing everything down.

If you're having a issue about your mother they'll record it. If you feel like they are not taking care of you the way they feel, they'll record it. If your mother used to claim that you were selfish, now when they are trying to influence you, or want to take control of you, they're going to take that from their Arsenal. They'll say, "even your mother thinks you're crazy." Or you are crazy? You don't even have friends , and you've got a issue with everyone. No one thinks as yours, yet you're the only one with this problem. It's not my fault It's from you".

They also will say things like. Have you been in a hospital? Are you feeling okay? Have you ever experienced a breakout before? Are you sure? You are quite emotional right now? Do you feel okay? These are all things to cause you to doubt the way you react to being victimized and they also want to have some influence over you. What you have revealed to them, and they have kept secret to you, they'll make use of the information against you.

Find your shame

One method to handle gazing in a relation is to to be being able to recognize your guilt and be aware of those instances when someone attempts to make you feel ashamed and uses your good name against you. It is normal to feel ashamed in that moment since you don't realize the fact that you've been victimized because the vagus nerves are taken over and you're being dissociated from the world. Vagus nerves receive all information from the outside world and stimulate you as your brain transmits information to the body in a similar way. This means that your brain is controlled while you're offline. In that instant you will not be able to comprehend that what's taking place to your body is a violation. You are unable to comprehend the event in perspective. You convince yourself that you're not employed to alleviate someone's emotional distress and you then tell yourself that you're reacting to the feelings and your brain is off. This is the real goal that someone is blazing a trail of gas to you.

The gaslighter's person will make you feel scared in order to be able to influence your emotions. You will feel like you're in a state of panic and make you begin to doubt your own reality and cause you to feel guilty for asking them questions. In the event that a man, or the wife of a man is a gaslighter and her husband discovers that she is engaging in an affair, she'll explain to him that it's his fault for catching her in a relationship. She will explain to him that it's his own fault for cheating but she didn't think that she'd become the woman who will be cheating on her husband, but it's because of her husband that she's engaging in the behavior she's engaged in. Even if a man is working more than one job, the wife is always complaining that he's not making enough money and that he does not have a nice home and a nice automobile. Therefore, the person she's cheating with will try to keep her feel happy. In addition, because the man doesn't stay home all evening to be attentive to her, she's got rights to leave with a partner and have a fling. Therefore, the man is totally sceptical about whether the woman's words are true.

So, a gaslighter usually uses a portion of facts to defend their victim. For the victim, he'll assume that since he's not home every day and that's why she's doing her best to cheat on him. The only thing he needs to do is say how many times he's been drunk and then explain what the motive behind his behavior is from. The woman will say that because he is working in two different jobs a time and isn't home every day, she has the right to cheat upon her. She might say, "it is your fault that I'm cheating on you because you are too tired whenever you come back home." If a gaslighter is exploitingsomeone, the victim is used as a tool for abuse, and there's a lack of compassion for the people in his life seeking to be feel happy. Gaslighters can be deceived.

She could say that I'm not involved in an affair. Try to convince her believe that this is all that this was on his thoughts as well as that the individual are only friends and that's why the husband let her have a companion she can hang out and have a drink with. She'll say that she's had this person for throughout her entire life, which means that he won't be skeptical about what he witnessed. She might say something like "how can you possibly think this about me? I don't go home every day and I don't have to spend the whole time in a lonely place. The husband might think that it's true "because I work every day I think it's okay to have a acquaintance at home to have a drink at all times. Sure, she takes charge of the children throughout the day long".

Therefore, he will continue claim all of these things as his friends and doubt it is his right to ask questions about the actions of his wife. While she's talking about all of these things, she is just lying to her husband's face. Gaslighting aligns the primary need for a person to lie, and to perform the act they want to do as well as exploiting the other. Thus, gaslighting throws to the other person can throw them off the balance. When you begin to increase your power in relationships, it's not common for the psychopath, or the narcissist gaslighting in order to throw you off balance. Gaslighting is a way of brainwashing. It's a good idea and you have a idea, you've got a reality , but the person you are with keeps making you think you're not saying the right thing.

He'll cause you to doubt whether you are entitled to experience an inner experience. If you accuse your husband of was cheating on a woman, you'll be able to prove it, but the gaslighter will inform you that you aren't entitled to experience that.

The Gaslighter may also reveal what you're wearing in that fragrance, and claim that he doesn't like the scent even though he has told you earlier that he liked the fragrance. It's a little moment that happens over time, and they attempt to educate you slowly to profit from you later on.

The purpose of gaslighting is to make you feel like a victim of emotional balance in order to make you feel like you're not able to find the courage to walk away from the relationship. A person who is gaslighting you will pick you up and then puts you in the corner. He's a bit strict but he'll straighten your hair and ensure you're in order. Then, while no one's looking the man will knock you off the Wall. Now you're launched into the air due to the fact that it's Humpty Dumpty. And often, the person who shot you will pick you up and say that he'll take the best care of you, that nobody will love you as much as the way he does, and that he's there for you because he loves you.

Even though you're broken and fractured, since the person who pulled you back up and placing your back against the wall you'll be inclined to join along with the person, and in the next few minutes the other person will push you back against the wall.

Triangulation

Gaslighters are known to employ triangulation. They will use triangulation to communicate in your home with your friends as well as with your colleagues. They'll attend a celebration in your face and say that they love you , but the problem is that you've been away lately. They'll say, "you forget things or that you are accusing them of things that they are not guilty of." They might say something like, "you came home last week and you have accused them of having an affair with his boss."

Because a psychopath sociopaths narcissist is aware of what you think and when they have an opportunity to bring your down, and cause you to believe that you're insane They will continue doing it since they are trying to get you triangulated. They'll place that thought in the minds of those who you know as well as the people you love to make sure that you don't do you have a family support network. You must be aware of this a sort of thing is happening in your life as it can be very destructive.

Lies

The Gaslighter is a liar who will lie to you and, when you inquire about it, they are shocked , and they will make statements that include, "how could you think of me? to add another level of insults to the mix.

Chapter 4: Caution Signs Of Gaslighting

1. They'll tell you the truth.

It's a Falsehood. But, they tell you this lie through a informal pronunciation.

Why would you think you're so self-deprecating? Since they established a fashion.

When they expose to you a huge lie it is difficult to determine if the information they provide is true. The aim is to make you in doubt and untrustworthy.

2. They claim that they never made any statement, even though they have proof.

You notice they made a statement that is specific; you are aware that you've have heard it. But, whatever they keep refusing to acknowledge it. This causes you to begin looking at your life and think "possibly they never said that." The more you think about this and you start to doubt your existence before you even acknowledge that it is true.

3. They make use of what is precious to you to serve as a weapon.

They understand how important your children are to your and also the importance of your character to you. That's why it may be one of their primary aspects they attack. If you have children They will inform them that you shouldn't have children. They'll say that you'd be a unique person in the event you didn't possess this list of bad traits. They challenge the very foundations of who you are.

4. They can wear you down with time.

This is a very nebulous aspect of gaslighting. It's done constantly and is then retracted after a period of time. An untruth now, a lie there, a untrue remark periodically... . And then it starts to produce.

In fact, even the most beautiful of people could be affected by gaslighting. It's that simple. It's the connection "frog in the skillet" The dish is slowly heated up to the point that the frog isn't aware of the problem that is affecting it.

5. Your actions do not match with your words.

If you're in charge of an employee that "works" with gaslighting, look at what they're doing, not what they're saying. The things they say amount to nothing, they're just talking. The way they conduct themselves is the problem.

6. They can reinforce positive things to make you confused.

Someone who must reduce you to a minimum and reveal to you that you've no value is now praising your accomplishments for something you've accomplished. It also brings a sense of fear. You may think, "Well, perhaps they're not unreasonably awful."

They are. It is a determined effort to lift you out of the shackles and to examine your life again. In addition look at a look at what you've been celebrated to; it's most likely that it has been a gift to the Gaslighter.

7. It is known that confusion reduces the strength of people.

Gaslighter is aware that people like to feel safe and familiar. They'll probably squelch the belief and cause you to constantly think about things. The typical inclination of many people is to concentrate on the person or the person who makes you feel more secure This could be "unintentionally" the Gaslighter.

8. You project.

In particular, they're drug addicts or fraudsters Yet they constantly deny it. It happens so often that you begin to defend yourself and become enticed by the real actions that is the gaslighter.

9. They are trying to convince people to oppose them.

Gaslighters are skilled in controlling and identifying people they know will be in their midst which is why they use the people they find against you. They'll make comments such as:

Someone knows what's wrong. or

The person who knows you're also ineffective

It's important to remember that this doesn't mean that the people who said it actually did say the opinions they did. Gaslighters are a consistently lying lie-teller. When the Gaslightner employs this method it is easy to sense that you aren't sure who you can trust or go to, and this leads you towards the Gaslighter.

In fact, that's the reason they require isolation: It provides them with greater control.

10. They'll tell you and others that you're insane.

This is among the finest methods for gaslighting because it repels. The Gaslighter recognizes when he speaks to your brain that people are going to be able to have a difficult time believing in your words in the event you show them that you're brutal or insecure.

It's an effective technique, and those who are close to a Gaslighter are completely ignorant in regard to this manipulative, controlling and sexist behavior towards them. The Gaslighter is adamant and exuberant about how much he loves his loved ones.

11. Everyone else is a lying liar.

When you are able to tell you that everyone else is a lying person This makes you think about your beliefs yet again. There's no one with the courage to reveal that information, so they must be honest isn't it? No. It's a method of controlling. It forces people to go to the Gaslighter to obtain an "right" data - which is a major lie.

The more you are aware of these methods, the more quickly you will be able to recognize them from the rest and avoid giving in to Gaslighter.

How to deal with the effects of Gaslighting

The term "gaslighting" (called "gueslaitin") is the term used to describe methodical control that takes place within the family, professional academic, strict, or environment. The person who is trained as a Gaslighter uses this method to convince their victim that they're negligent or deranged in a certain event over time. In this way, the person is in charge of the person in the situation in.

A good model is one who constantly accuses you of how you think about things or how you perceive reality, even though you clearly remember the details. They may do this to avoid issues they prefer not to consider, but after a while the repeated assertion that you're insecure or overcompensating and never correct can cause your confidence and conviction disappear. To recover from gaslighting and in managing the belongings of your home it is important to change your mindset, regain your faith and establish an encouraging group of individuals.

1. The effects of gaslighting

Getaway . Controlling yourself is a mental and psychological mistreatment with the sole purpose of being in control and controlling you. If you are in the event of such a relationship, it's best to look at it again and decide if it's worthwhile to continue with someone who has done this. In that case, would you be able recover.

For example If you think that you have recently realized that your accomplice does things done in a way that makes you think about your own motives, that is the most important reason why you must be removed from the relationship.

Talk to someone intimate about how you can escape from this particular situation. Speak to a sibling or friend that you're being controlled by your partner and that you must to break free from this relationship.

* Speak to a specialist or another expert in emotional health for advice on how to end the process.

* Reach out to a supportive group of people to report any instances of uncontrollable behaviour at home. They will learn how to manage you and give you different contacts that can aid you.

Reduce stress levels . Stress can connected to a significant amount of stress and cause stress, anxiety, and fatigue, as well as other negative results. One way to improve your self-image is to try to control the negative emotions and eliminate their causes. Certain smart ideas include yoga, meditation breathing exercises, perception.

*There are a variety of ways to ease pressure such as yoga, care and so on.

* Imagine yourself in a serene place and add subtleties, such as a image of you with your jaw and your temple fully relaxed. You can see the smile all over and the happiness in the eyes of your.

Make sure you take care about your stress . Stress and anxiety are the results of being gaslighted. If you're honest it is no longer a matter of confidence in yourself and spend every ounce of energy worried about getting blamed on something that you did not do. This can be an example. In order to get rid of it, you must find ways to calm yourself.

For instance, in the possibility that you do not know what you look good in on you , due to the fact that your partner constantly scrutinizes your clothing, and asks thoughts and asks questions, try to get over this fear of being disappointed by them.

* When you feel that your anxiety is raging try to calm yourself by focusing on the steps of treatment, allow yourself to feel the tension for a moment, and then take note of what you feel without making a a an assessment of yourself, and let the anxiety go.

Focus on your breathing, and consider "in" when you take in and "out" when you inhale out. This can be helpful in the midst of anxiety attacks.

Make sure you take care of depression . Being a victim of mental illness and out of control often brings sadness as a consequence. If you are in any way, remember that you have the power to combat it. Look for signs and then try to overcome them.

* For example, take note of whether, throughout the duration of your relationship you

had issues with finishing simple tasks weak, or losing energy and enthusiasm for a long time.

Check if you are experiencing physical signs that could be interpreted as gloomy regardless of whether or not you think it is. Things like shifts in appetite or rest as well as physical ailments, unexplained discomfort, lack of focus or concentration, etc. could be clues.

Seek out professional assistance to treat and recover from demotivation. This will help you in making the decision of whether to take prescriptions or go for alternative medications.

Create strategies to fight sadness consistently, such as by creating a motion routine, but not getting in the return. It is wise to stay clear of alcohol and other substances.

2. Restoring Confidence in Yourself and Others

Take note of yourself . It is an extremely challenging aspects of your recovery and, more importantly, the most important. As you are constantly monitored it is common to disregard your body's instincts and eventually disappear, however, this can be reversed.

Start by doing small things, such as paying attention to your body, do it in the instance that you are feeling tired or agitated and tell you, "I can believe myself to know when I have to eat or rest. That may not appear anything, yet it's a major advance toward your fearlessness."

When you must make a decision, don't be limited or grant this power to anyone else. Say, "I know my time, and I want to discover what every one of my alternatives are before I settle on a choice."

* Rehash "I can confide in myself and my judgment" whenever you begin to doubt your own judgment.

Visit the site that gives you information . One of the effects of gaslighting is the tendency to doubt yourself and others about your mental health. When under control, you could even go to an extreme that you will accept what your partner says regardless of what other people say. After you have recovered, you should try to restore your faith in others by looking into the source of what people declare.

Begin by trying to build confidence in a couple of trusted people. Select a person who's just had to experience his lows and highs with you as a close friend.

Use them to determine what's real and what's not. For example, if your friend says that you're beautiful, inquire whether she's honest or is lying.

Keep a journal . One method to recover from mastery is to write it down at any time something that inspires you to have confidence in yourself happens. A journal filled with these experiences can help in proving that other people are trustworthy.

* When you have made a option and it proves the right choice, write it down! Discuss the time you decided to carry an umbrella to take on a sunny day that was a windy day.

Also, note the instances where people prove that they're trustworthy. For example, if you have a friend who promised something, and actually did it.

Utilize affirmative statements to yourself . It's not difficult to a victim of a gaslighting attack to feel depressed, lonely and lonely, since this is certainly a doubt the intention of the perpetrator. Build your confidence through positive self-talk.

* Write down your diary's characteristics and then receive a part of the words

Utilized in the rundown to talk with your self.

Instead of rehashing the fact the fact that you're apathetic or neurotic, instead, tell them that you are

Insincere, claim that you are competent to be creative, innovative, and committed, and repeat, "I can trust and such as myself."

You should spend your time doing activities that you like. You might have missed those things you've always loved, particularly in the case that you were required to look after your former partner. Make sure to carry on the routine that inspired you to heal.

* Try to take at least five minutes each day to do something that alters your mood For example, you could prepare to sing in front of the mirror prior to going to work.

* Do something you haven't attempted in quite a long time, for instance, playing the piano, or one or two exercises to refresh your memory, and determine if you can are able to go back to the thing that you were interested in.

Be sure to take proper care to take care of yourself . The constant gaslighting could make you unwise in due to it being a intention is to make you think that it isn't making a difference. You'll require energy and energy to recover to be healthy, so focus on your health.

Do some physical exercise such as yoga, hand to fight, day to day walks and so on.

• Eat healthy meals as well as snacks for energy and a positive attitude.

* Take a good amount of sleep. If you want to be able to face the battle and restore faith in yourself, believe in your decisions and make decisions confidently It is essential to stay energized. In that moment, it be possible to stay on track and maintain self-control.

3. The creation of a support network

Find professional assistance . Recuperation is quicker and more efficient in the event you have a team of people that who you can count on. Doctors and specialists are tuned in on what you want to say and will provide useful tools to manage the effects of gaslighting. They also can be involved in people suffering from sadness as well as nervousness and stress.

* For example, in the event that you were in an unbreakable relationship that you

were able to be controlled in a reliable manner An expert could assist you in identifying the consequences of these ill-treatments and how you can handle them.

It doesn't matter if the relationship that was referred to was short, speaking to an expert will help in understanding how to recuperate.

• Talk to someone whom you trust about the incident. Find out who is able to influence you. Experts or HR professionals school administrators, and so on could provide you with great advice.

They can aid you in managing adverse effects of depression or anxiety. They can also help with other problems.

Rely on your family and friends . This advice is particularly helpful in the event that you've been unable to keep yourself from a group of people during gaslighting, and believe that no one else is thinking about your situation. In most cases, the perpetrator can convince the victim that only they know what is the best for them and this causes the victim to isolate away from their friends and family. Make these connections again and admit the fact that these people are a part of your recovery and that you have the ability to confide in them.

* Contact someone near to and invest time with them. You don't have to be done.

Nothing fancy such as going out, but it's

Encouragement to spend the evening in your home and do nothing.

* Recognize invitations to social occasions from friends and family. Begin by taking a small amount of time in the class. A trip out for coffee or a small snack is a great starting point.

Participate in a Support group . Join with fellow gaslighting victims as you take a look in to the stories they have to tell (numerous similar to yours) and also the advice they have to offer for managing the recovery process. Positive collaborations from a care group can increase their confidence as well as create connections.

* Look for instances of domestic violence victims and the like in your immediate vicinity Request proposals from people close to you, the researcher and your personal pioneer etc.

* Join online gatherings as well as discussion about it on possibility that you're unable to meet face-to-face or in the instance that you don't find a group to participate in.

Chapter 5: Building Space And Healthy Borders

Now you know that you're a person who has been gaslighted. You also know that the most important first step in recovering from gaslighting is cutting yourself off from the person who is causing you pain. You might have finished the final chapter feeling depressed by the thought of segregating yourself from them. Since the person who abused you has systematically indoctrinated you to question the truth of who you are. It is clear that they hold a tremendous influence over you and regardless of whether or not, it is clear that you are dependent on them in various ways. That means the thought of leaving them could trigger huge amounts of anxiety. The first thing to remember is that this is not uncommon. Then, realize that you can turn the energy of your stress to positive things. This chapter is about making use of your energy to gain authority over the events of your day. The first step is to create the distance you need between yourself and the person who abuses you. Then, it's important to establish boundaries that keep you from the power of your abuser for good. This chapter is also helpful in different situations. You might need to go back to this chapter while you seek out other positive relationships. It is important to establish boundaries therefore, make sure you use these tools constantly as you seek to regain your freedom and your life.

Cutting Ties and Moving On

You're ready to admit that you've been gaslighted, and you're eager to make your life complete. You are not completely free of your abusive partner. You are able to live without your abusive partner. Here's how to get started.

If you're in a state of panic at the thought of ending your relationship with your abuser immediately effects, then there are a couple of steps you could do prior to leaving to ease the transition and help you get an emotional break with your victim.

1. It is important to look at your abusive partner in a different way. Get out of the relationship for a time, and think about whether they're the kind of person that you would like to surround yourself with. Get rid of all the negative past, erase all memories, and instead consider whether they're a pleasant individual, a nice person a pleasant person. If you can't perform this task on your own as a stranger, imagine that someone you love is in a relation with the person who is your victim. If they truly are gaslighting your feelings, you'll be shocked by the idea that they are manipulating and abusing one you cherish. You must then return to reality. If you don't desire that type of relationship with someone you like then why would you choose to accept this for your own? You deserve more. You ought to want more for yourself and not feel embarrassed about it. If you're able to admit you're a deeply flawed individual who has abused you repeatedly and repeatedly, then acknowledge that it's time to change your life to something more positive. There's no

shame in seeking more from your life. Eliminating the aforementioned a major obstruction is the best method to not only achieve happiness but also to happiness.

2. When you've discovered a method to recognize the terrible character of your abuser You may be overwhelmed by uncertainty and indecision. It's normal however it is something you need to overcome. In order to find the path out, you need be able to understand why you stuck around in the first place in the first place. Yes, your abuser may have created you as a victim however they could have also done something that led you to remain. Consider taking a moment to write down everything they've done to make you desire to remain with the relationship in your lives. This might include things such as paying attention to finances, offering support or compliments, praising and flattering you, and so on. There are a myriad of things that they've employed in order to feel happy enough that it's difficult to let go. So, instead of attempt to give up the benefits right away

and then make a plan of how you can find the advantages in other locations.

If there are financial advantages but how do you be financially self-sufficient? Do you have someone in your life that can offer a credit until you attain the independence you desire? If the financial gains are substantial and you'd be broke and homeless if you didn't have your abuser, then you'll need to locate a center or group or a family member who is willing to assist you in finding an independence even when it takes time. It's not easy to let go, however it will make it easier to know that you have a strategy instead of taking a uninformed leap.

If there are emotional support systems that you'll miss take a look back at your support system before they separated you. There are others who have stood by you in the past and it could be other people in your life to contact. The person who hurt you made you believe they're the only person who could ever bring you joy There are likely to be plenty of people around you who are willing to listen to you and assist you in these difficulties.

If you have other benefits such as affirmations from friends and the feeling that an partner can make you feel loved and/or attractive, then you'll have to seek out a different source: you. It might seem contradictory or perhaps naive but the truth is that you've not been able to love yourself enough to leave the toxic relationship. If you do not discover how to be happy with yourself then you'll most likely get back into the cycle. Don't try to get approval only from others. Be yourself and be awed by yourself. Write down the things you love about yourself, praise yourself, and take pride in your own achievements. There will be upcoming chapters with specific steps to achieve this, however you can begin with a small amount. Take a look in your mirror directly to yourself, and say to you, "I love you." Continue to do this until you truly believe it.

3. Your feelings are involved in the person you abuse. That's how gaslighting is done. You've been deceived to a position where you are able to trust only them or yourself. Another way to identify the abuse and try to escape is to reflect on the emotions they create. Following every interaction with them, take a moment to think about it, and then record. Are you feeling positive, negative, or and numb? Do you feel overwhelmed, confused, and guilty? Did they ever say anything that boosted your confidence in you or increased your self-esteem and happiness? If you're feeling slighted What you'll see is a pattern is emerging. You will experience some good levels, naturally however, the majority of the things you're experiencing will be depressing and feeling draining. It provides undisputed evidence which links your feelings of sadness and anxiety directly to the person who is causing it. It's hard to ignore and accept that the one that is meant to be loving and/or supporting you is in fact beating you down instead.

4. It may be difficult to find someone who can be able to replace the good things that the abuser did for you However, that doesn't mean you should quit. Others aren't the only solution. As we discussed in the previous chapter your abuser may have eliminated you from the activities you enjoyed in the past. As you try to get rid of the assault, it's the time to revisit those previous delights. Perhaps you were able to draw, write or dance, sing or even play a sport. While not involving the person who abused you make a plan to try these things repeatedly. Simple actions like these are a ideal way to show you that there is a way to feel content with no one else in your world. They can also demonstrate to you that you can be independent. Your happiness shouldn't be contingent completely on one person. It is important to accept that you are able to be content with yourself.

5. One of the most effective ways to avoid the temptations that come with a negative relationship is to begin building a strong one. It could require some thought and

time However, it is important to find people you believe would make a good acquaintance. You should look for a someone who's inspired you to laugh and smile or seems to have a number of things in the same way as you. You can now increase the positive impact of those experiences in your relationship by spending more time this person. Invite them to a cup of coffee, or go to a film or participate in something you know you both like. If you can build that solid base, it will be much easier to speak with them about your daily life and what you need. What you'll experience is a entirely different experience from what you experienced with your victim. You'll have a perspective that allows you to state that this new relationship is superior to the one you had with your abuser. It will also allow you to recognize the imperfections in the abuser's claims of love and support.

6. One strategy you can employ to succeed in a change in diet similar to a method to use to get rid of a unhealthy relationship. This method is to allow yourself to indulge

in one thing at least once in a time so that you don't feel satisfied. Of obviously, you shouldn't always take pleasure in foods, however this could be what works best for you. If you're able to stay clear of your partner go on a date. Take a trip to one of your most loved places. Request a partner to take part in a exciting thing with you. You can stay in and enjoy a kind of spa-like day. You always punished yourself for being with your abusive partner. Now is the now time for you to give yourself a reward when you are able to stay away from them. It is a good idea to increase the difficulty in time. For instance, you could begin with a reward by not speaking about them for an entire day. This may sound like nothing however it's much more challenging than you imagine. When you've completed the day, make sure you do something you love. It will become easier to stay clear of these thoughts for a entire day, try to try to stay away for three days before receiving the next reward. If you continue to build your endurance this way eventually, you'll be able to last for months, weeks or even years, without speaking to your abuser or letting them interfere with your thoughts constantly.

7. The final suggestion is to go on a break and then return to your home after breaking relations with the person who abused you. The exhaustion that you experience is likely to manifest in physical manifestations which is why you should make sure you take a day to rest, sleep or relax. Rest is a time of healing and to reflect. This is exactly what you require to be able to leave and get out of the abuser relationship.

Building Boundaries

The steps listed above are not going to work If you don't be able to stick by setting the boundaries. Boundaries will prevent you from falling back into traditional patterns that allow abuse go on.

One method to establish a solid limit is to create something you can quantify. It doesn't mean you need to draw a diagram of the relationship, or something similar to that. The best thing you could do is apply the information you've gathered by analyzing your abuse and select the most egregious and consistent assaults you've experienced. Imagine it's a series of insults that tell you the way you look to others because you have allowed yourself to go, yet the abuser is there in the end. When you've had a conversation to your abuser note down everything you remember the conversation. You can then go back and see the times they have were negative in the discussion. Consider how it affected you. After you've gotten a handle on your feelings when you engage in a conversation in which they try to put you down , respond clearly and concisely conveying your thoughts. If they are unable to acknowledge or express what you are feeling, they've violated your rules. Get out of the situation immediately, so that the person who is causing harm will not be punished for breaching your sense of security. After that, record what transpired in the incident. After a while, you'll have a record of the numerous occasions they've strayed from your boundaries without regret. This means that they don't respect or admire you enough to pay attention to you when you establish the boundaries in the first place.

Certain boundaries are more concrete as emotional borders. If you feel overwhelmed or surrounded by your partner, physical distance and a limited or no contact could be the ideal solution.

To establish physical boundaries In order to establish boundaries physically, you might require something that is as easy as asking your partner to take a step back when you converse with them. This could be as extreme as dissociating yourself from the person's presence completely. To determine what type of boundary is most suitable your situation, you might prefer to begin with a small physical border and see what effect it causes. If your abuser responds in a significant way, then you're probably in such a unhealthy relationship that you must get rid of them completely.

If your abuser is struggling with the boundaries, but is able to honor it in the slightest way, you could remove yourself from them less gradual. This can be more convenient for you, but it can make it harder to leave. The best approach is to keep a constant ear to your emotions and determine what will enable you to achieve the freedom and happiness you desire faster and securely.

To make contact with a limited number of people It is recommended to mix the first and this one. Create a boundary that is measurable such as allowing one telephone call a every day, or sending texts only between hours of 9-11. In the above paragraph you must determine what you are able to take on emotionally, and also the reaction of the victim. Reduce the frequency of contact if you believe you're not able to live without contact or accelerate the process of limiting contact, or simply go into no contact when you feel comfortable or feel uneasy.

Boundaries are most beneficial because they're not only being quantifiable but also being regularly implemented. You must be accountable in some manner. It could be through the creation of a chart or journal to monitor your improvement. You could also do this through appointing an accountability partner that will continuously be sure to check in to see how you are doing and offer feedback when you begin to slip. Consistency is essential to your freedom and being consistent will help you set boundaries when you're looking to establish a an entirely new and healthy relationship.

Chapter 6: Why Gaslighting Mechanism

Gaslighting is a way to eliminate any doubts about one's abilities and also any previous experiences that could make the victim be too "damaged" to see reality clear.

Gaslighting drains a person's inner resources which means they're not able to self-validate and ultimately fall into a feeling of helplessness they've learned.

Gaslighting can deplete individuals of a solid sense of self-worth and the certainty of their perception of the world.

* Gaslighting generates anxiety and fears that were never there, and causes the victim to dwell on their own shortcomings rather than the transgressions of the abuser.

The person who was gaslighted is compelled to look into whether the person responsible has done something wrong instead of focussing on the conduct of the perpetrator as the reason for concern.

* Gaslighting can cause survivors to fail regardless of the actions they take. Abusers are able to show disapproval no matter how hard a victim is trying to please their victim. If victims remain still and obedient or become aggressive and aggressive and assertive, they will be punished. In shifting the goalposts, the perpetrator can change their expectations and assertions at the drop of a cap.

* Gaslighting distracts from it, denies, rationalizes, and minimizes the harrowing acts of physical and mental violence.

* Gaslighting can be a risky form of retaliation to victims who speak out, as each time they doit, they face a physical or mental assault that makes them feel depressed and weakened.

REAL LIFE SCENARIOS OF GASLIGHTING USING RELATIONSHIP AS A CASE STUDY

1.Perhaps the most frequent usage of gaslighting is a manipulative spouse in a pair. People in the relationship may claim to others that they are in affection and love however it's anything less than. The very act of this method of manipulation is a way to block true feelings of love. The manipulative and controlling partner may add a bit of gaslighting into conversations early in their relationship. Maybe the last time you met them, you had agreed to do something on a Saturday and then mention it later in a text or over the phone, they revert to the original plan:

"No, silly, I said Sunday. I am occupied throughout Saturday."

This is a relatively innocent line and you shouldn't think about too much since you're in the stage of being captivated. You could dismiss it in the belief that you've just misunderstood or remembered incorrectly. Such a thing, in isolation, doesn't necessarily mean that you're being misled. It could be that you actually not understand, or spoke in a different way without intention to. If this type of miscommunication develops into a common occurrence you must begin looking for the reason. As time passes you could notice additional contradictions between the statements at various times in time.

2.You might propose going out for a meal at a Mexican restaurant on a night because your gaslighting partner once told you that he really liked Mexican food only. You could get this reply:

"I'm not a huge fan of Mexican, but I know a great Thai."

Are you mistaken? Did someone else claimed they enjoyed Thai food? What happened to their story from then to the present? If you're certain as you can that they had a desire for something and then change their mind and say they didn't in the future, it could be their method to put you on the wrong side of history and making you feel like you're not paying to. If the gaslighting gets taken further the perpetrator will try to make appear as if you are now reversing what you had previously said. Depending on the time that you've been an issue for, they could or might not confront you about it in the first place.

What should you do when you've got a gaslighting acquaintance?

The first thing to do is stay clear of them. One option is to openly discuss it and quit. Remove all ties to them and tell them that you don't would like their services, and be certain about your decision. It could be a difficult decision but if you need to eliminate their harmful influence, it's crucial to get them out of your life. Don't just wait until the gaslighter is exhausted of manipulating you and dismisses you. You're more valuable than you think! Do you really want to wait until they've lost interest in you? Why should you let someone take over your life with unneeded drama when you could make a difference?

Another option to end the relationship is to be boring to be around with and make the gaslighter is able to leave the relationship. Gaslighters are known to cause people to be frantic and confused If you react to them with a skepticism and unsure, they will tire quickly and get their eyes off of you. Instead of being defensive in response to an angry comment made that is made by a fellow gaslighter respond by saying "Oh, I see," "Maybe," "Okay," and then on. Be thoughtful and consistent And soon your gaslighting buddy will think you boring as they come.

Whatever distance you are to a person who is a liar If you choose to put an end to the bullying, make your mind not to take anything from them, or loan any money, in particular. Refuse any gift or any assistance they provide. The gaslighter is always looking for a method to make their supposed gifts return to haunt you. They could take it to the point of accusing you of stealing the gift from them. This is just one of their numerous methods of getting to the point where they believe that you've committed a wrong. If you loan them something, don't expect to receive it back. Do not exchange anything with them, to keep yourself from a negative reaction.

A person who is gaslighting you doesn't really care about you or everything that is important to you. Never leave them in the charge of your children or pets as well as your belongings. Gaslighters could cause irreparable loss to you. Even worse, they could refuse to admit they did anything wrong and convince you that they're all in your mind. An unintentionally slanderous friend could blatantly claim to be the cause of something they are certain did, then blame you for making false accusations. They might say something such as, "How could you jeopardize our friendship by making such grave allegations? Your wild imagination has been allowed to become out of control and I'm not going to sit there listening to this absurdity!"

Protecting Yourself From a Gaslighting Family Member

If you find that you're unable to accomplish something good in your family, no regardless of the effort you put in you might find that you are being manipulated by someone (your parents, siblings or even other family members) is shaming you. This is a common occurrence in families that have different standards for rewards and punishments. In these situations, a particular family member (usually a "golden child") is given the highest treatment and , even in the event of a mistake and are punished, they receive a lesser punishment. However those who are the "scapegoat child" always gets the most savage treatment, and their accomplishments are rarely recognized. In reality, their shortcomings are often exaggerated over the top to make them feel off-putting. If the scapegoat child is ever in a battle between the child who is golden they are usually blamed for the entire thing that occurred. The victim thinking, "How exactly is this my responsibility? Are I missing something Is there a conspiracy going on or is my mind slipping away?"

A common scenario that is played out in gaslighting among families is the drama triangle. It is when there's a the victim a persecutor as well as a rescuer. A persecutor (the gaslighter) is able to oppress the victim by intimidation and threats. The victim needs a person who is a rescuer (a non-biased third person) to aid in the rescue of the victim from being in the fire of the person who is being persecuted. For instance, if you are the victim of the family and get involved in a battle between the gold child it's going to require a neutral party to end the issue in a fair way.

However, it is possible to be treated as a victim by the rescuer not intentionally. In the case of a rescuer, for instance, when he is called in to settle a dispute and then to pacify both sides, they will declare, "No, that didn't take place. It's just a matter of taking meanings out of it. Put it all behind and get on with your life." It could be that they have been able to end a conflict, but they have also undermined your emotions. You're sure that you're not taking any significance from the behavior of the other person however, every time you interact with them, you're being told that you're just imagining it. It could eventually cause you to begin to wonder if the issue lies in your head.

In addition, you cannot live your life waiting that someone else will be there to help making you feel like you're complete or unfinished depending on the situation. You must take the necessary steps on your own to safeguard yourself from a rude family member.

You can prevent yourself from being slammed by a friend or family member through choosing your battles with care. The relationships between siblings and the relationship between parent and child is very different from the friendships and relationships of spouses. It can be difficult to leave the family member who is causing you to feel slighted. However, you have the option of choosing to try to make a argument with them or avoid them, especially if you're not able to stop living together within the same household. By significantly reducing your contact between them and you lower the chance of conflict.

Do not doubt yourself or your memories , regardless of the opinions of others. If you must deal to a parent who is a gaslighter, whether in a way, or not, disengage yourself from their presence whenever they attempt to gaslight you. Beware of conversations and discussions that may school to disputes.

Being able to protect yourself from gaslighting from a family member doesn't mean you have to be averse to the person. Maintain a healthy respect for each family member, but be sure to maintain respect for yourself. Don't allow others the opportunity to look down on yourself.

Protecting Yourself From a Gaslighting Spouse

Perhaps the most difficult part in safeguarding yourself from a gazing spouse is to acknowledge the abuse. It's a difficult job for many to be objective and logical when dealing with those who are close to their hearts. The love they feel for someone can cause them to overlook a number of offenses. Also spouses of abusers may stay longer in the relationship that is abusive as they are unable to recognize the reality of what's happening. Thinks like, "No, it's not feasible! He's too sweet to even think about hurting me." "She has always been with me throughout all the way. It must be insane to think she would ever want to hurt me." continues to force victims to endure the violence.

The first step you should make to prevent yourself from gaslighting is taking a a honest and objective view of the situation. Remove yourself mentally from the situation and examine the behavior of your spouse. Do you notice a sequence of unhealthy behavior? If yes, then take immediate action.

You should be able to get out of the relationship in the event that you do not want to. Do not let anyone drugs you to believe that you are unable to live without them, or that they will remain in a relationship for longer than you would like. If the person who is gaslighting you threatens your safety, don't do it lightly. Inform the police immediately.

In fact, gaslighters can be great people who have an emotional wound that require to heal. But you're not a counselor, and neither is it your duty to begin diagnosing mental health issues. You must fix yourself first. One most secure way to accomplish this is to put the most distance you can between yourself and the person who is causing you to gaslight. If they're narcissists, or not, find yourself in a good place before you offer to help.

After breaking off through a gaslighter, never turn your back! They're likely to return after you to try and reestablish contact, but you shouldn't give the chance. in Chapter 7 we'll look at a look at a sneaky technique that gaslighters and emotional abusers employ to lure back their victims into abusive relationships. For now, let us declare that when you are ready to bid goodbye for a gaslighter, shut the door to your heart and throw away your keys! Do not make acquaintances with them. Don't be deceived into thinking, "We're no longer together, but we can still be friends."

Based on your relationship with others It is a good idea to be closer to those whom you depend on. However, do it in the spirit of seeking out support, not looking for someone else that you can trust. The views of third parties are fine but your personal opinion is valid. If you make the choice to safeguard your self against a gaslighter, you must have the faith that you are able to handle every other obstacle life may present to you.

Don't forget that you don't have to be averse to them. Instead, think of the time you spend with them a opportunity to learn. Learn from the lessons you've learned from your relationship to become a more rounded person. Get rid of the need to hurt them and get them off. If you do, it will be clear that they're in control of your thoughts.

Chapter 7: The Rotation Of Gaslighting

This is the reality gaslighting takes place in a pattern. It's a technique of manipulation, together with brainwashing, that is employed to make people doubt the person they really are and then become less confident in themselves as well as perception and, of course, identity.

Most of the time in the milder cases it is a odd power dynamic that doesn't work in relationships. The person who is gaslighting is dependent on the actions of the one gaslighting, and frequently when it is at its most extreme, it's close to control of the mind, which is not good for anyone.

There are seven phases for the vast majority of the time, those who are gaslighting suffer through. Below will be a discussion of what these stages are.

Lies And Exaggeration

This is typically the first thing you do after having been smashed up enough, usually by praising and false words. The person who is gaslighting you will make negative remarks regarding the person being gaslighted. Usually the comments are about you being insufficient, or have a flaw in your. The comments are based on generalized views instead of a objective, verified factual assertion, which can cause the person gaslighted into a defensive position. Most of the time, this is exaggerated and embarrassing as well like the mother yelling at her daughter for not putting things on the counter at checkout prior to her doing. The daughter may say it is because she "hates it" but when asked, she will typically fabricate an imaginary fairy tale that isn't very relevant.

Repeat The Process

Most of the time, this isn't carried out in one. Though, I wish it were. The majority of people won't repeat it once because they know that once isn't enough. Actually, they'll continue to do it since they are aware that it is psychological warfare as the lies continue to be made in the hope of being active, so they will remain in control. You cannot do it all at only once, instead you repeat it many times in order to become dominant in the relationships you are in.

The Escalation

Each time anyone is challenged and they don't be able to back down. Actually, the gaslighted will escalate the situation every time there's a possibility of challenging it, as they triple and double down on the attack, meaning that when you challenge it one time it will be challenged repeatedly and ensure that it gets more and more difficult every time.

Each time you try to blame someone else for something they'll say no, regardless of the thing they say or do. They'll also disprove any evidence is a final, false assertions in an attempt to mislead the individual, or blame. This means that you'll be held accountable for whatever it is they do.

What's interesting about this is that the people who engage in this behavior believe so strongly that they didn't commit any wrongs and that they are the righteous ones in this situation, that they can be seen in full view in the moment, and then afterward, they'll attempt to disprove the claims you make. For instance, if you tell them that you had a relationship with a different person and they deny it by claiming that it wasn't the case or get to the point that they'll call you names about it.

They'll ensure that it happens again and again and the problem will get more difficult on the part of the victim the longer time passes.

Wear The Victim Out

They'll continue to go with the attack until you're exhausted. The gaslight will wear away the victim as time passes. The victim will become disillusioned, pessimistic, depressed as well as depressed. They will also be unsure of themselves. The victim will realize that they could be in the wrong and begin to doubt their own perception of reality and their own sense of identity and perception.

It can last for a time. This occurs a often, and is something a number of people encounter over the course of time. People will experience this struggle because they are aware that as they battle with their gaslights the situation will get more difficult.

This is especially true when the person who is being slighted is one who is a self-deprecating narcissist, too. They'll do it because they are aware that they'll slowly attract the attention of the other and take this action because they will make the victim feel a bit numb. This is where the next step comes in.

Codependent Relationships

It's a relationship that is built on emotional and psychological dependence on another individual. In essence, you're dependent on your partner nearly completely until the point that you are unable to think for yourself and you're forced to emotionally and psychologically rely on someone else.

It's not a healthy relationship and in reality, it's incredibly harmful. At the point that the gaslighting will cause the person who is being gaslighted always anxious and insecure about this. The gaslight will, also, render the person incapable of relying on anyone else other than the gaslight that will make the other person pull the strings.

The person who is being gaslighted is in control here. The head honcho who is able to provide acceptance and respect, as well as security and safety to the person that is gaslighted. The person manipulating frequently has the ability and can at times be so confident in this regard that they'll do everything they can to get away this power. The codependent relationship is, of course unhealthy and they depend on the vulnerability and rejection in order to build it so that one cannot ever be free and has to rely on the other in order to move forward.

The False Hope

This is a manipulative tactic that allows the person being gaslighter can appear a little nicer to the person who is being gaslighted. This allows the victim to show a superficial sense of kindness or a conscious of their actions or a little moderation However, it's a false impression. This tactic is in the first place because the victim is then conditioned to believe that the person who is being gaslighted isn't really so bad, isn't it? This is certainly something that could have been worse.

Butthat's not the reality. This is a false belief. The idea of this is making the individual believe that it's a good idea to stay there. However, it's only a show is put up. They're in the real world not likely to alter.

The goal of this tactic is to fool you. They are aware of what they're doing It's a deliberate move designed to create a sense of complacency in the people who are being targeted.

They're asking you to put your guard down and if you fail to do so it, you're opening yourself to further assault. They'll want you to keep your guard down prior to being gazing again. This can also increase the likelihood of codependency because you feel that you're dependent on them.

Sure, they can be charming for a moment and they might even offer you gifts and make nice gestures however, you shouldn't be relying on it.

It's a temporary step in order to expose you to the next gaslighting. As we've stated in the past, they'll never ever stop. They will never give up until, of course, they are in complete control.

Control Is The Goal

Control is the aim It's a quite extreme degree of control. It's not just that they have control over a few aspects in every aspect of your lives. The people who employ gaslighting will have control over everything they have the power to. The goal of those who is using gaslighting is to control, dominate, control and profit of others, or, in certain cases even the entire society present. If this continues and accelerated, it will just keep going.

You've been beat down by this person which is why people think it's the sole way to go.

It's not. But for those who have been victims of gaslighting, they're subject to the pressure as well as lies and false hopes that are set in the first place.

The person being manipulated is the one who suffers the most. The fact is that all you'll experience is anxiety, fear and doubt over every incident that has occurred. The person who snarks at you will exploit you as often as they can and the reason is personal power and gain.

Narcissists have the power to influence your life, among the outcomes of a Narcissistic gaslight is doubting everything you do. It's not simply a handful of things, the whole thing is what you perform in your life, and everything that occurs in your life. If you decide to embark on this road, it will damage your self-esteem and that's what the gaslighted narcissist wants.

When it comes to relationships, this usually means that the person is dependent on the person who gaslights constantly having to follow the rules of the other, which can be detrimental to you too. In relationships, you have the least amount of freedom in life. And you'll be aware that with this and the fact that you're not going to be able to leave until you take the right steps.

We'll go over the steps to end a relationship with gaslight in it. We'll be able to discuss a couple of the signs of gaslighting that can occur in the event of negligence and what could take place if you're in this situation in the following chapter.

It's a pattern of controlling and you should never think that the person who is being abused will improve. They don't grow and don't improve and you'll end up in the path of hurt and suffering if you persist with these types of abuse. Avoid the pain and heartbreak and take the right decision for yourself.

Take control of your life, your health, and get started taking action right now, before it becomes worse for you.

Chapter 8: Why You Need To Prevent Gaslighters

The recognition of gaslighting as the psychological abuse that it is, will allow you to eliminate it when its signs start to show up in a relation. A person in a Gaslighting-related relationship can be harmful to you in every aspect : physically, mentally, and emotionally. It can cause a mess in your mind and can cause you to lose the core of who you are. It's possible that you need to stop your gaslighter due to the following reasons:

They mess up their victim's Head: Nothing is more painful than losing your essence. Your unique being. These particular characteristics that define you as "you". That's the way that gaslighters behave. They sabotage their victims' heads and leave them questioning who they are. This is a horrible situation no one wants to confront himself or herself. If you leave in the early stages in the relationship will cause them to lose their influence on you. Avoid trying to argue with them. Diplomacy isn't among their strengths.

Don't Let Their Victims Feel Guilt The Gaslighters employ the guilt-trip technique. It's an emotional manipulation technique that they employ to manipulate their victim. They make their victims feel trapped and feel guilt over and over. They aren't sure what the feeling comes from, but this is because the gaslighter appears to be the victim.

They abandon their victim in A state of shame After all the undeserved criticisms, there is a feeling of guilt. The victim is left feeling accountable for the misdeeds that are taking place in their relationship. Absolutely not a ideal situation to be in. He is aware that this anxiety will wear confidence in yourself, which is why he continues to smear you.

They reduce your self-esteem and Self-Confidence. The main warning signs to watch out for in gaslighting victims are low self-esteem and a complete loss of confidence in oneself. After being misled often by the gaslighters their self-esteem has been severely diminished. They are now convinced that they are just not good enough. The longer you hold onto a gaslighter in order to restore your self-confidence as a result, the more you are being attacked. The only way to help yourself is to let go of their grasp and leave the toxic surroundings.

Feelings of Depression: Victims of gaslighters always feel depressed. This is due to a persistent feeling of being lost in the process. They feel less joyful. Sometimes, a lot of good events could be happening at once, but they aren't feeling as satisfied. They're yet to gain the respect of someone who they have become a fan of, so they feel like they're failing.

Feelings of hopelessness: The victims of abuse through gaslighting are suffering from intense feelings of despair. There could be a myriad of positive things happening in their lives, but it does not help their cause in the least. There's also a feeling of numbness toward everything going on in their surroundings.

Feelings of anger: They feel anger at their gaslighters, families and friends. Everyone is affected by their anger. They are angry at their fellow victims as they are responsible for their abuse , as well as to family and friends since they feel dejected by them. It's a feeling of abandonment.

Suicide: Abusive behavior in relationships is among the reasons why suicide occurs. Being slighted can leave one with a feeling of desperation. In these cases, people are feeling like their lives are not worth living and they have no hope of getting to get out of their troubles. The most effective way to get out is suicide. to get out.

Chapter 9: Defensive Yourself Against Gaslighting

If all you have learned about a nation and its citizens is the result of a single book that you have read, it would not be prudent to draw conclusions about that nation or its citizens based on one story. This is how gaslighters function. They point out a flaw (that may or not be true for you) and attempt to convince you believe that.

The gaslighter selects a single tale that you have lived through and plays it repeatedly until you believe that it is true. In choosing a story (usually a negative one) and then playing this story in a loop that your attention and focus are focused on that negative part. The instances where the gaslighter's false story appears to be true will begin showing up and eventually, you'll consider the truth of the narrative.

A gaslighter doesn't have to be in a intimate relationship with you in order to gaslight you. They could, for instance, include your supervisor, subordinate or even a coworker, however since gaslighters can direct their attention to your performance, their impact could cause a significant amount uncertainty in your capabilities. Gaslighters generally are not interested in the complete destruction of your beliefs, rather they tend to engage in the dismantling of your opinions and convictions. While they may not be able to directly criticize you however, they can accomplish similar results through "being realistic" about what you can and cannot do. They'll repeat the tale of your inadequacy until they are convinced.

The most dangerous thing you can do to yourself if you suspect you are being gaslighted is to fall into denial. You have to listen the gut this is precisely the thing that the gaslighter will never want for you to think about doing. This chapter provides helpful advice you can follow to keep yourself from falling for the lies that gaslighters offer to you.

Protecting Yourself From A Gaslighting Coworker

If you believe that someone has been snooping around at work, the first step is to confirm the fact prior to making any decision. You shouldn't act too fast only to find out that you're just imagining it.

Here's how to be sure that someone is attempting to influence you through gazlighting in your workplace. If you are always overworked, either to show your worth or due to being tasked with tasks that fall outside the scope of your duties (and often shaming) You could be suffering from gaslighting at work. If you are made to feel unqualified by deliberately making you feel unqualified, or assigning you dates that are not correct to force you to be late, or are unable to comprehend what you are expected to do

114

You are exhibiting strong evidence of gaslighting.

Another subtle indication to watch out for is not turning down opportunities because you don't like them , or because you don't feel qualified, but to avoid being judged. A coworker who you believe to be at odds with you if you answer yes to an opportunity is likely laughing at you. They might have shown frustration at the way you've been doing in the workplace, shouting insults as they walk through your office, mock your actions in front of their fellow coworkers, and trying to appear unprofessional in front of your boss. To prevent more emotional attacks You begin to slide back from your shell and allow them to control your work behavior.

There are other items to keep an eye out for:

* We will not be able to exclude you (from essential meetings and gatherings with coworkers).

Always linking every conversation with something you didn't do right in your past.

* Making comments that are sarcastic at you when you raise a complaint. For instance, "Obviously, you have a problem with following instructions."

* Spreading false reports about you.

* Disagreeing something they've claimed to have said.

If you observe a continuous pattern of a negative behavior from your direct reports or boss, coworker or a different employee you can think that they are blaming you.

The next step is to keep a note of your official interactions. Keep a record of every instruction or communication, and be sure to keep backup copies of all electronic and written communications. If communication is verbal and you are unable to get a witness or ask them to record the message in writing (where feasible). For instance, if your boss who is a gaslighter is in a happy mood, suggests that you get a day off after you finish the task at hand It's a good idea to ask them to record the request in writing while they're in in a happy mood. It's hard to get gaslighters to make up a quick swoop on you if they have evidence that is concrete. If they refuse to acknowledge or attempt to deceive you, you have evidence to support their claims and preserve your integrity and self-confidence.

If the gaslighter continues in their conduct If they continue to behave in a way that is unacceptable, you may report them the matter to Human Resources or higher-level supervisors. Make sure you have evidence that is irrefutable (paper or digital evidence) prior to filing the official complain. It is also important to follow established procedures when the process of making complaints in your workplace. You do not wish to find yourself in breach of any lawful rules while trying to defend yourself.

Although speaking to a handful of other employees at the office to determine whether they're dealing with the same issue, it can be helpful but it might not result in your favour. A person you speak to could be a snitch and cause things more complicated. There is a chance that you will be accused of gossip or gossip, and that won't be true. If you have to speak to others in the workplace about the issue Be sure to know who you're confiding with.

Another effective way to protect yourself from future attack by a gaslighter , is to communicate clearly with them. Tell them that you are aware of what they're trying accomplish, and that you are not prepared to play with them. Gaslighters often try to conceal their tricks but exposing the fact that they're hiding in the open can help make them feel less vulnerable. As an example, instead of engaging in absurd arguments using defense phrases like "I did not," or "I am not," formulate your remarks in encouraging ways. It could be something like, "I refuse to argue with you. What do you really want and how can we accomplish this together?"

Gaslighting isn't limited to intimate relationships by itself. It occurs in work more often than we would like to admit. Don't let it happen because you're trying to avoid conflict. Take a stand and don't let someone other than you to convince you that they are a person who is a slack.

Protecting Yourself From A Gaslighting Friend

Your circle of friends could be a powerful source of support that can help you in times of need. However, they may also become the source of your anxiety by establishing a pattern of backbiting, vilification sharp criticisms, shaming and guilt-tripping. Because we're conditioned to expect support, love and integrity from the people who are closest to us. It could be difficult to recognize the signs of manipulation from friends.

The shaming of friends could make you feel ashamed for your decisions and dissociate you from those who could help you feel confident. If they keep beliefs that you are superior to theirs, they are able to control you in any way they like. If you feel you have a need to create a acquaintance with you, even though they constantly make you feel lessthan, they already control you.

If you find yourself constantly looking for a person to take the decisions for you, then you must seek their permission prior to making any personal decisions or you think you're unable to make any decisions that are that's acceptable to others (keeping up with the latest fashions) with them, but you're not completely content being with them, then you might be staying a person who is a snob as well as a "frenemy."

You're dealing with a gaslighting friend when what you share with them in confidence turns into a matter for the public to consume and ridicule. Someone who gets pleasure from gossiping about you and is enthralled by your mishaps is showing indications of gaslighting. They'd want to meet you in a battle with other friends, a fight they initiate.

What do you do if you've got a gaslighting acquaintance?

The first thing to do is stay clear of them. One option is to openly discuss it and quit. Remove all ties to them with them, inform them that you don't would like their services, and be certain about your decision. It could be a difficult decision however, if you have to get rid of their negative influence, it's crucial to remove them from your life. Don't just wait until the gaslighter is tired of manipulating you , and dismisses you. You're worth more! Do you really want to wait until they've no need for you anymore? Why should you let someone distract you with their drama when you could take action?

Another option to end the relationship is to make yourself boring with the people you hang out with, so that the gaslighter will quits the friendship. Gaslighters love to get people angry and off balance If you react to them in a manner that is ambivalent or unsure, they could tire quickly and take their eyes away from you. Instead of being defensive over an angry comment made that is made by a fellow gaslighter respond by saying "Oh, I see," "Maybe," "Okay," and then on. Be thoughtful and consistent And soon your gaslighting buddy will find you boring as they come.

However close you may be to a untrustworthy friend If you choose to stop the abuse, you must make that you will never borrow anything from them, or loan them anything, particularly money. Refuse any gift or all assistance they provide. The gaslighter is always looking for a method to make their supposed gifts return to haunt you. They could even go as far as accusing you of taking the gift from them. This is just one of their numerous methods of getting angry with you if they believe that you've done them wrong. If you loan them money, do not expect to receive it back. Do not exchange anything with them in order to keep yourself from a negative reaction.

A person who is gaslighting you doesn't actually care about you or everything that is important to you. Do not ever let them in the charge of your children or pets as well as your belongings. Gaslighters could cause irreparable loss to you. Even worse, they could claim they never did it and convince you that the whole thing is in your mind. An unintentionally slanderous friend could blatantly refuse to be accountable for something they are certain did and then accuse you of having acted wrongly. They might say something such as, "How could you jeopardize our friendship by making such sweeping allegations? You've let your wild imaginations take over and I'm not going to sit there listening to this absurdity!"

Protecting Yourself From a Gaslighting Family Member

If you find that you are unable to do any good in your family, no regardless of the effort you put in It is likely that some one (your parents or siblings or any others in your family) are shaming you. It happens frequently in families that have dual standards of reward and punishments. In these situations, a particular family member (usually a "golden child") receives the most favorable treatment, and even when they're not right the get a less severe punishment. However"the "scapegoat child" always gets the most savage treatment, and their achievements are not recognized. In reality, their shortcomings are often exaggerated out of proportion , making them feel off-putting. In the event that the scapegoat kid is ever in a battle between the child who is golden they typically take the blame for the entire thing that occurred. This could leave the child who was the scapegoat contemplating, "How exactly is this my responsibility? Are I missing something Is there a conspiracy or is my mind slipping away?"

A common scenario that is played out in the gaslighting of families is the drama triangle. It occurs when there is a the victim a persecutor and a rescuer. A persecutor (the gaslighter) may ostracize the victim by intimidation and threats. The victim needs a person who is a rescuer (a non-biased third person) to assist them in saving the victim from being in the conflict with the person who is being persecuted. For instance, if you are the victim of the family and you are involved in a dispute between the gold child it is going to take a neutral party to end the dispute in a fair manner.

Unfortunately, you could be treated as a victim by the rescuer inadvertently. For instance, when someone is called in to settle a dispute and also to pacify both sides, they will declare, "No, that didn't take place. It's just a matter of trying to interpret meanings from it. Put it all behind and go on." It could be that they have been able to end a dispute, but they also affirmed your opinions. You're certain that you're not interpreting any meaning from the actions of another person, but every time you speak with them, you're informed that you're imagining things. It could eventually cause you to begin to wonder if the issue is really in your head.

Furthermore, you shouldn't have to wait around that someone else will help you making you feel whole or complete or whatever the case. You must take the necessary steps on your own to safeguard yourself from a unkind family member.

You can avoid getting a rude response from a friend or family member through choosing your battles with care. The relationships between siblings and that between parents and child are completely different from friendships or those of spouses. It can be difficult to walk away from the family member who is causing you to feel slighted. However, you have the option of choosing to try to make a claim with them or avoid them, especially if you're not able to stop living together within the same household. By greatly reducing the contact between them and you reduce the likelihood of conflict.

Don't doubt your memories , regardless of what others tell you. If you are dealing in a confrontation with a parent who is a gaslighter, whether in a way, or not, disengage yourself from their presence whenever they attempt to gaslight you. Beware of conversations and discussions that could pharmaceuticals to disagreements.

Beware of being gaslighted by a family member doesn't mean that you must be averse to the person. Maintain a respectful relationship with each person in your household, but make sure you respect yourself. Do not give others the opportunity to look down on yourself.

Chapter 10: How The Gaslighting Narcissist Operates & The Habits They Will Attempt To Make You Believe You Are Wild

There has been a range of studies that focus on gaslighting, and the effects it can have upon a person. What was discovered is that there are seven different stages that are typically utilized by a gaslighter who is narcissistic in order to gain control in the eyes of a person. It is crucial to keep in mind that the circumstances vary, therefore the amount of stages or sequence in the order in which they occur may differ.

We'll examine each step of gaslighting. The more comfortable your experience is with the phases, the better prepared you'll be to deal with the situation. If you're already in a relationship with a manipulative narcissist It can be a struggle to grasp the events that are going on around you. The details that follow will help shed some insight into the situation, making the ability to think on your own and free yourself from the toxic relationship that is a relation with a gaslighter, much easier.

The first step of gaslighting involves exaggeration and lying. The use of lies and exaggeration is to force the victim into a protective position. The gaslighter will attempt to get the victim to believe there's something wrong in the person or they're not good enough in the way. These claims are not grounded in reality, but through repeated use and repeated use, the victim will begin to believe in what the narcissist says.

Some examples of phrases that could be used are:

You're apathetic person Everyone should be aware of how much of a fool you are.

What does it mean that your work is essential? It's a unnecessary waste of funds and time for you and your business.

I can't imagine the way your work can be justifiable.

What made you fold your clothes this way? I've said to that to you a million times how much I dislike it when you do this. What's going on?

The next step is repetition. When we hear the repeated lies or exaggerations repeatedly and over again, we're constantly in a condition of defensiveness. In addition, it permits the gaslighter who is narcissistic to remain in the offensive posture. They can maintain the control over every aspect that is part of their relationship. This will not only ensure that the victim remains in the defensive posture however, it is likely that they'll begin to believe the lies that are repeated over and over. They'll begin to wonder whether the negative remarks being stated about them are actually true and, in the end, if they continue to hear it and they believe it.

The third stage occurs when an escalation takes place when the gaslighter is questioned. If you attempt to face the truth that they're lying the situation become more ugly. The narcissist will begin to attack you in a more aggressive manner in an attempt to regain control. No matter if you have any evidence, or even if you do, they'll counter the claim. They will resort to blame denial, denial, or false accusations to make you feel confused and to bring you back in check , where they believe you are.

The fourth stage is when the gaslighter attempts to take their victim's place. The gaslighter who is narcissistic will always be in the forefront that will reduce the victim's energy.

The victim can become discontented and numb and self-doubting. and possibly debilitated by the constantly abused. It is typical for those who are constantly gaslighted to doubt their own sanity and their reality. For some this may happen fast; for others, it's a longand slow process. The more solid that you feel in your self-esteem and your convictions, the longer it takes to bring down to submission.

The next step is the formation of a dependent relationship. If we're codependent with our partner it makes us feel like we cannot accomplish any thing without them. This is a reliance that is too much on the other person. If you're in a relation with a Narcissist who employs gaslighting strategies that are constantly employed, they will attempt to cause you to feel stressed and unsecure. If you do that, they're strengthening the bonds between you, and encouraging codependency. The victim eventually is likely to seek approval, safety as well as acceptance and security from the one who is causing the gaslighting. They will then have all the authority. The codependent relationship is often founded on fear and vulnerability that are two factors that a gaslighter who is narcissistic will attempt to exploit.

The 6th stage is where the gaslighter with a narcissistic personality gives false the victim with false. This is a method of manipulating. The narcissist becomes milder and more angry with his victim in a brief period of time.

The victim will feel like there's an underlying faith that things will change and improve. This tactic is often employed against the victim when they begin to recognize there's a issue, or when they begin to assert themselves. When the gaslighter notices this, they'll take a carefully planned move to ensure that their victim remains where they want them to be. If this strategy works and the victim is more comfortable, and may allow their guard to fall, which is extremely risky. This can strengthen the codependent relationship , and also allows the manipulator to progress into the seventh stage.

The last stage occurs when the narcissistic gaslighter gains absolute control and dominates the victim. The gaslighter is ultimately seeking to be in control and dominate over another. They would like to profit of their victims. Through constant gaslighting that the victim will be regularly in a state of anxiety or self-doubt and anxiety. The victim's feelings are utilized by the narcissist in order that they will gain total control and authority.

How the Gaslighter Will Try to Make You Think You are Crazy

After we've gone at the different phases of gaslighting, we'd like to talk about the strategies a gaslighter with a narcissistic personality will employ to make you believe you're insane. It's extremely frustrating to know that there are people in the world who take advantage of other people in this way and therefore, understanding the signs of mental and emotional abuse is crucial and will ensure your pain a healthy and happy life. If you're in a partnership with a gaslighter with a narcissistic personality It is crucial to understand these indicators to be able to recognize that you aren't insane. They're simply trying to make you feel this way.

The strategies used by the gaslighter for making you appear insane are usually quite subtil. They attempt to undermine your perception of reality and also your belief in your self-worth. They attempt to appear as if you're the one who is the one with a issue, or that you are the one who messed things up. Let's examine a number of different ways that the gaslighter could be able to say or do that makes you doubt your own sanity and reality.

The first thing they could do is to discredit you.

They attempt to appear as if you're being insane or unstable when you are in the company of others. It is possible that they also try to do this when you're one on one. The more you're discredited and criticized, the more likely to begin to believe you behave irrationally or you're unstable.

They are also known to be their assertiveness confidence, assertiveness, as well as faux compassion, to convince victims that they've made a mistake. Through this method, they create doubt in the victim and they begin to believe the gaslighter's version things. The longer this continues the more likely the victim will start to believe that they suffer from memory problems and that the gaslighter is always right.

Change of topic is another tactic that someone who is blaming you for something will attempt to make you feel insane. They'll quickly attempt to switch topics by simply asking questions. They might also make comments that directly affect your life in a negative manner and aid in gaining control. Examples of the statements and queries they might make include:

Why do you keep imagining things? Nothing has ever happened.

It's not likely that you're remembering it right.

What was the source of that wild idea? came from?

The narcissistic gaslighter can also be great at minimising things. They'll try to make your feelings seem insignificant. This helps them gain more influence in relationships. A few examples of how they can minimize the intensity of your emotions are by using phrases, statements, and words like:

Why do you feel so sensitive?

Why are you angry? I didn't do anything could be considered to be a cause of this kind of a reaction.

Do you not see that I was just joking? It's always too easy to take things seriously.

Avoidance and denial are two other methods that gaslighters employ to make you believe you're crazy. They'll be unable to accept your thoughts, feelings and thoughts. This could cause doubt within those who are the victims. Some examples of what they could use to justify avoidance or denial include:

It never happened, you probably dreamed it up.

Why would I ever say something similar to this?

Stop from lying.

Stop shifting the topic.

I don't know what you're talking about.

The final tactic we'd like to explore the gaslighter who is narcissistic may employ to make you feel insane is the twisting of events. They'll subtly change the words or twist the words of someone else to make it work in your favor. If this happens in this manner, it's likely to make the victim think twice about their memory. The most common method is attempts create a feeling of being insecure or unsteady. Some of the phrases that can be used to describe your narcissistic partner will try to twist the truth of the meaning of what they said or did include:

This is not what I've said. I was saying _____.

If you can remember the details, it was like this.

What do you think it means to see it this in that

The methods that gaslighters employ to make you feel insane could differ. Here's a good overview of some of the common actions that they'll try to perform. If you've got a thorough understanding of the issues you're facing You will be prepared to manage the situation in a way that does not result in being afflicted by psychological and emotional abuse. If you're suddenly doubting your mental health, it might be time to speak to your family members and friends or a professional so that you can take back the control over your life and the happiness you enjoy.

Chapter 11: Symbols That You Are Being Gaslighted In Your Association

Being gaslighted means, you are being disempowered. If you're in a relationship which is causing you problems or you're not content in your relationship, this means that you're being gaslighted. Let's discuss the signs you've been gaslighted as well as the things you could do if you're a person who is a victim a victim of gaslighting.

Being told lies by the person

The first reason is that you are continually being lied about by the spouse. It's normal that your partner will make up stories at times, but if it is a continuous thing, it means that you've been lied to. If this happens your spouse may tell you something at the moment and at the next moment, they switch it to something else. One day he that he loves Chinese food, but the next day he claims that he likes Mexico food and isn't a fan of Chinese food. Most of the time, the lies he spreads aren't huge. They're just small falsehoods that he says every day. This is a excellent sign that you're being deceived and being misled.

He doesn't keep his word.

The other sign is when your partner is not keeping his word. This is when he says he wants to right now to do something, but after a while, he alters his word. For example, he might say that the time is 2 p.m. but then the time is five or six p.m. So, arriving home at 5 or 6 pm isn't at all the issue. The issue is in the moment you speak to him and inform the man that he stated that he would be at home within 2 p.m. Then you will hear him say that he isn't sure what you're talking about. They will make people feel like you're insane. They will say that you're out of your mind. They will inform you that they have never stated that they'd be at home by 2pm, but they'll be back when they can. You have heard that they would be home at 2pm, but they're not.

They might also claim that they are going out with their friends this evening to shoot pool but then, later on you'll find out that they weren't with any of the boys, but were in a dancing club. When you confront them, they'll tell you that they didn't say that they were heading to a pool, but they did say that they're going out. They might run into their friends and then shoot a tiny pool but later they'll head out to a nightclub. All they do is designed to make you believe that you're crazy, insane or that there is something wrong with you.

The goal is to make you continually feel guilt-stricken about yourself. They wish you to feel ashamed about yourself. They continue to tell you that you're not worthy. For months after committing the crime and they continue to make you feel guilty about the act. They make you feel guilty and unworthy They keep saying something like "it was your fault, you did it." If you weren't guilty it, we'd be with each other for years. If you hadn't done the thing, you'd have been content. They constantly make you feel unimportant and inadequate. They tell you that they don't think you are worthy of you.

But, you must be able to convince yourself that you're worthy. You must. Don't let anyone say that you're not worthy. You are a flying eagle who is in flight towards your goals and dreams. You are self-deserving. You're worthy of loving the body with sincerity. You're worthy of confidence. You are worth respect. This doesn't mean that you're perfect, or that you aren't prone to mistakes, but rather that you're worth it. Do not be afraid to tell anyone that you're not concerned.

Their actions and words do not coincide.

The other indication could be that the just words and their actions do not match with each other. They may say something, but then do the same thing. For example, they will tell you that they love you , and that they would like to have a lasting relationship with you, however their actions do not match the words they're declaring. They'll tell you that they love you however, they'll continue to go out with a different woman or a man, or continue to do things that cause you to feel uneasy. They'll refuse to engage in any actions in your direction in the pursuit of their hopes and dreams or whatever their goals and dreams were.

Utilize positive reinforcement in order to confuse yourself

The other indication is that they attempt to use positive reinforcement in order to get you confused, and appear as if you're crazy. If they tell you how to behave and what they will do with you need to do, they immediately begin bombarding you with affirmations. They will continue to shower you with positive phrases to keep you from falling off. They continue to make you leap between one foot and the next, and you're not sure which foot to land on since the moment they're giving you positive reinforcement but the next they are saying that you're a nuisance or will continue to lie to you.

Convince yourself of their actions

The other sign is when they continually accuse you of what they're doing. It means that they do something wrong but then are back accusing you of doing the exact identical thing. It's a way of saying that if they can accuse them, they could accuse you as well. However, you are, in contrast they are accusing them since they committed a mistake however they accuse the person of an accusation that isn't truthful.

They are now using the tactic of turning the tables by shifting the blame on you in the process of accusing you doing the exact same things that you are accusing them of. This defeats the entire argument and reduces your credibility. They also try to use people to hurt you. They use your family members against you. They make use of their friends to harm you. They take advantage of your parents to hurt you. They use your brother to harm you. They make use of your sister to ensure that you are controlled.

All they have to do is to find enough people to place stress on your from various ways, such as themselves as well as your own guilt and feelings of unworthiness to the point that you fall to the floor and do the advice of others, just like a humble servant following the leader.

Inform everyone you know that you're crazy.

The next thing to do is they inform everyone that you're insane. They tell everybody that you're a beautiful girl the first time they first met you, but after a few minutes, you went completely crazy and he does not even know what had transpired to you. You are now completely insane. Your friends will tell you that you're insane. They will tell your acquaintances that you're insane. They'll even tell complete strangers and family members that you are suffering from a mental illness. They will inform all people they meet that you have bipolar disorder. (As when there's something wrong with you having bipolar. Even great musicians

146

can be bipolar). This can make you feel anxious about having to receive a diagnosis from different doctors. This means they'll make you gaslight them in a way which makes you doubt your personal beliefs, and the things you believe in and the person you are.

How do you deal with this

To begin, start by taking a long, deep breathe and take a deep breath in air. Inhale in the air only and strengthen your mind by meditative.

Spend some moment away from the gaslamp and in your private space. Walk in your park. Relax close to a tree or in a room you can lock and switch off the lights, then remain there in peace and peaceful. Visit the backyard at the right spot and just be silent. Have a break at lunchtime And meditate, then start by breathing. As you breathe, you will find your center, you should then reaffirm who you are. Find out who you are. Make affirmations of I am to boost your confidence and strength and integrity.

Make yourself feel confident and honest. You must affirm that you're reliable. You can tell yourself that you're being rewarded. Remind yourself to affirm the affirmations from a positive perspective, rather than from a downward angle. Don't convince yourself that you're not crazy, instead, tell yourself that you're grounded. Try putting affirmations to the ground by placing some dirt on your feet, to help you utilize it to strengthen your own inner world.

Try to do daily meditation. Make sure you don't doubt your morality or core beliefs. Even if a thousand people in your life adhere to your beliefs, stay true to your values at the core. Be true to yourself all the way to the bottom of your soul in front of your eyes. You already have a sense of who you are, so it's not necessary to rethink it.

Rely on your judgment

It is the next thing to do: put your faith in your intuition. Belief in the information you receive. Believe what you hear. Be sure to trust every decision you make. Be sure to not let someone else use the things you love or that you consider important to you. The gaslighter will take the things you consider important, as do your children, and then uses it to harm you every day. You should not let this occur to you. The Gaslight might say something similar to however, we can enjoy a good relationship even though you don't have a child. You can enjoy a good relationship if we handed him over to his father, so that we can concentrate upon our relationships. Most people do this because he has said that you can both be in a excellent relationship if you offer the child to him as he would like you to gift your child. Do not let this occur. Make sure you value and safeguard your treasured possessions. You might also hear something similar to how we are likely to enjoy a good relationship when you sell your house and then use the money to travel. It is a clear indication that you're being deceived.

Don't allow that to happen unless it is one of your hopes and dreams prior to meeting the person. If you do decide to sell your home you cherish and you travel your heart desires, the decision must be based on your own personal feelings. It must be based on your deepest desires and desires.

Seek Professional Counseling

The second step is to seek out professional advice. Narcissists are likely to make you gaslight them. Therefore, try to find a professional who is knowledgeable about gaslighting. The fact that someone claims to be a professional doesn't mean you must hire him right away but rather, consider asking him questions by asking him "like are you able to demonstrate a adequate understanding of what gaslighting and are you aware of how to tackle it, since you're in a very difficult position in the moment. You need help in resolving the issue and you require an alternative person to speak with. You've got the same sharp, clear, open mind. You require someone who will be able to articulate your worth and guide you increase it.

Chapter 12: Considerate Narcissist

Since a period of time a certain level of narcissism was thought to be a prerequisite for a good self-image and one should love yourself to appreciate other people. However, these traits have now become common in people who have a problem with their character and then cause a lot of problems which are, in no way, comparable to others.

Narcissistic personality traits are common in the majority of people, but less than one percent of the cases are believed to be totally developed narcissistic personality problems.

The main thing to consider is an expanded mental perspective wherein the person sees themselves as exceptional appreciated, successful, and praised. Since the establishing of the elevated mental self-view can be a delicate process, an person is also prone to scrutiny. Additionally, there is an absence of empathy that is clearly expressed.

Self-overestimation and pretenses can transportation to despair and depression since one cannot be acknowledged by others as having an inflated view of oneself.

Narcissistic characters are often extremely marginal or introverted characteristics that create a tangle in the treatment and image of the adverse side effects.

What is a Narcissistic personality disorder?

The narcissistic personality issue is a disorder that affects about one percent of the population with a greater prevalence in women than men. The symptoms include excessive self-confidence, a lack in compassion and a profound reverence. Gaudiness is a key characteristic of a narcissist. We value wealth or notoriety and believe that extravagant treatment is justifiable.

It is not wise to compare a Narcissistic character issues with someone who is confident. Someone who is confident isn't a problem, but the narcissist doesn't have the ability to be humble. They're pretentious, egotistical and ignore the feelings and needs of others. Additionally, the problem negatively can affect a person's life. In all in total, person may be unhappy by their circumstances and confused by the fact that people don't value their achievements or offer them unorthodox service or attention. Each and every important area is in some way influenced (work or personal), social ...), however, individuals don't comprehend the impact of their actions on their relationships in a negative way. People aren't happy with a self-centered person They are also dissatisfied in their jobs, their public behavior, and so on.

Narcissistic characters are those who appear in the beginning to be optimistic, kind, charming attractive, decent and respectable ... However, the "narcissistic deviants" as they are often referred to (no sexual undertones here) are actually those who experience the negative effects of an utter lack of confidence frequently, but are not conscious of it. They exhibit a completely different exterior.

In this way, individuals, who have no self-control, feel superior to others, they should be respected and idolized and do not spare a moment to hurt the people in their vicinity.

Causes of Narcissistic Personality Disorder

The reasons behind the narcissistic character problem are not well understood, as with any mental problem, yet experts claim that it begins in the teen years. Certain circumstances can trigger it like:

Inability to understand and comprehend the feeling of empathy.

Implementation of a protection plan to protect against injury and misuse.

There is a lot of interest and concern from parents (significantly more so because of a one-on-one child).

Parents themselves are self-centered by not offering different guidelines to their child.

Refusal to befriend and/or dismiss acquaintances (at school or at home).

A lack of respect and friendship.

Some experts have suggested that a genetic or neurobiological problem may also be present, however there is no proof yet.

Who is affected by the narcissistic disorder? What are the risk elements? Men are more likely to be affected than women by the narcissistic problem.

In addition, people with low confidence, as well as those who are really desperate are at a greater chance of developing a Narcissistic personality issue.

In the vast majority instances, it's the underlying issues in the youth population that are the root of this problem (see the reasons.)

Contagion

A character flaw that is narcissistic isn't infective.

The primary symptoms of narcissistic narcissists

The indicators that define the narcissistic personality disorder are altered. There's no need to be these negative consequences. Narcissistic individuals can in this way:

Feel happier than everyone else around them

Change their mood frequently

Believe that everyone is unhappy and admires them. Tell lies to achieve their goals.

Seek out the achievements of other people.

Always seek acknowledgement.

Don't show any compassion to the those in their vicinity.

Be manipulative.

You should be serious and longing.

Not endure analysis.

You should be proud and haughty.

Doesn't matter to anyone other than the individuals

They are important to them, and who value them.

You are in control.

Refrain from any outside assistance or advice.

Believe that your companions (companion or companions) are blessed to

You've heard of them.

It's not unusual for those with an narcissistic personality disorder to misuse drugs and alcohol, suffer the negative effects of depression (counting self-destructive thoughts) and face significant issues with their relationships.

Characteristics That Define Narcissistic People and How They Can Be Identified

It isn't easy to organize a person who has a personality that is narcissistic, but many clinical studies reveal a section of the main aspects of this type of confusion. Take a look at a couple below.

1. Feeling of awe

Narcissistic people act and talk like they're a part of the planet's most elite group of people. This is evident in the way they interact with others. It's not necessarily aggressive (regularly not) however it is based on the notion that each has the upper hand, and that another has to respond to the other.

But not all narcissists can transmit their sense of being a rock star in a obvious manner. Some people possess a very specific and atypical appearance. Through all these conditions the predominance of opinion relies on the possibility of a future in which force will be maintained that will crush others, and in generating outrage towards the people who are seen by their social structure as having a better reputation.

2. They are easily annoyed

Narcissistic people are angry when things go wrong quickly, rapidly. This is due to the fact that with every disappointment they'll seriously damage their positive self-image they attempt to keep by their actions and relationships with the world as well as other people.

3. They strive to be leaders

Another characteristic of narcissistic people is their desire to take control and embrace initiative in order for the reality to be as perfect as they can with their self-image. It's not that they're more innovators in the end, but that they're seeking to avoid the mental tangle of having a lower level of job while recognizing they're more superior than the others.

4. They are self-conscious and have low self-esteem.

It might sound odd However, underneath the breastplate, people who are narcissistic have more instability that are visible in their view that is different from the other. This is why they're extremely confused when they aren't given their due consideration (which is a huge amount to be able to fulfill their expectations).

Therefore, their self-concept is a win-or-lose issue: a glorified mental self perspective is often dismissed as a fact but even the tiniest contact with reality causes a mess and puts in the same line all assumptions regarding oneself.

5. Stories are created to prevent making mistakes. Narcissists are unable to admit an error, and also avoiding displeasure by seeking absolution.

In this way, they place blame on other people, and reach an extent where their disappointment over a decision taken is seen as an obligation of someone else who's not present, for example buying a item or product of poor quality, with which it isn't possible to perform effectively. Often, the displeasure of not being able to create a fake story in the moment about the reason why someone else is at blame for your actions could modify to a greater discontent and anger.

6. They are extremely concerned with the aesthetics and appearances

The rest are constantly made by narcissists therefore they require a simple and simple method to accomplish this. In general, this means they have a significant amount of attention to the appearance of people: the clothes they wear and their style and style, and other things. They do not have to judge more those who meet the fashion standards more, but prefer to assign a lot of "character" and "character" to those who meet the requirements.

161

7. They manage their image a great deal on social media networks.

When it comes to filtering the pictures they share on social networks such as Facebook They are extremely cautious. Apart from the fact that they like having numerous "companions" connected (in light of the fact that having many creates the impression of widespread regardless of whether they're recognized or not) They only show the pictures of individuals who have been through a period of deliberation. They also use image altering tools to fix certain photos, while claiming not to detect them.

8. They take everything personally.

They believe that whatever happens is a part of a fight for attention. This means that they're frequently surpassed by someone else, regardless of whether or not they choose to please the majority. The narcissist may feel degraded in the circumstances and might employ assault tactics against another, but rather than directly confronting them.

9. They are not aware of the notion that "constructive criticism."

It's untruthful for unreliable people to take into attention to their errors and failures. This way it's not good to believe that these studies will aid in making changes in the future.

Chapter 13: Narcissistic Abuse?

Narcissistic partners are involved in the systematic manipulation as well as devaluation and manipulation of victim which leaves the victims with a feeling of inadequacy or anxiety. They can even selective to suicide. This form of continuous coercion, which involves a cycle of idealization-devaluation-discard violence in which they "lovebomb" their spouses, devalue them, and discard them before the trauma starts again, is known as narcissistic abuse - abuse by an NPD partner or on the other end of the narcissistic continuum. This kind of abuse could result in permanent emotional and psychological marks.

.In actuality, experts in trauma Pete Walker (2013) suggests that frequent emotional abuse can result in signs that are a sign of PTSD and Complex PTSD especially if the abuse was experienced in childhood and later repeated in adulthood. The psychotherapist Christine

Louis de Canonville (2015) is also addressing the concept of Narcissistic victim syndrome in her novel The Three Faces of Evil: Unmasking the Whole Spectrum of Narcissistic abuse. What makes narcissistic violence particularly dangerous is the fact the fact that they employ tactics that are delicate and manipulative to influence their spouses. Due to the nature of their behavior and the fake identity they project to the world at large they are able to avoid accountability for their actions - which is usually a beautiful mask to conceal their abuse.

Important to know is that narcissists aren't killing them directly in the way physically abusive spouses can They are creating the seeds in your brain that can anxious your life to be destroyed. They may incite fears that didn't exist, create anxieties that were never there and rub salt on wounds they are aware that you do not want to reveal and all this under the pretense to "helping" you or gassing you into believing that you caused or received the violence.

Most often, they alter the crimes they perpetrated to make you sound as if you were the victim you were.

Narcissists can reveal a confusing combination of debilitating lows and highs in an effort to keep your attention on the substance they abuse. The kind of behavior they employ can be so subtle, that many victims don't recognize they've been manipulated and some are only able to recognize the tricks in a relationship with a abusive narcissist after 10 years, whereas some are lucky enough to be aware of the issue early in their relationship.

Narcissistic abuse can lung to toxic behavior. These may include but aren't restricted to:

Unnecessarily critical and coercive toward spouses, judging their spouses in private and public by threatening verbal abuse and manipulative tactics that are used to deter them. This may include name-calling insulting remarks disguised as jokes, insulting comments that are snide regarding the character of the victim's intellect or line of work life style, set of skills achievements, or other social networks that provide support outside the marriage.

Physically or sexually. This could include hitting the person with furniture hitting or shoving, scratching the victim, making threats, or moving the victim, forcing the victim to engage in sexual activity without permission, and forcing an individual into sexual situations in which they aren't comfortable. They may in any way threaten to remove the victim, or even destroy his or her life should they do not fulfill their demands. Inducing violent or hostile situations in which the victim is subjected to emotional stress, particularly due to the narcissistic rage of the perpetrator over seemingly minor or minor issues. The perpetrator creates an environment in where the victim feels insecure, uncontrollable and limited in what they are able to do or say.

Engaging in both cold and hot actions that effortlessly switch between a compassionate and a violent person. It can be a pattern of violent behavior known as idealization, devaluation and dumping. This involves treating the victim without any apparent reason or reason, and then treating them rudely and coldly then returning to loving and affectionate behavior using a method known as repeated reinforcement. The victim will be conditioned to feel less confident and less each time they interact, it can also teach the victim to associate love with uncertainty, anxiety, and discomfort. This is followed by the person being disregarded in a humiliating and demeaning way, usually coupled with a attack on the victim that makes the narcissist believes that they've "won" the breakup.

Involving in every aspects of life for their spouse until they are able to isolate them from their friends and family and sabotaging the relationships of the victim's families, important occasions in life, or even their goals and hopes.

They will entrap their victims in the privacy of their homes should they ever raise any concerns regarding the relationship and exposing the victim to a series of silent abuse and disappearances in the course of abuse to create a feeling of vulnerability in the victim, making the victim be on eggshells in their efforts to please their abuser.

Triangulating their victims to others who are also lovers, such as ex-partners and friends; engaging in the most egregious deceit and manipulation as they engage in multiple relationships and comparing the victim with others regarding their appearance, character and other traits to create a belief that they are not worthy of their own the victim. This behavior is not caused by the primary partner's anger, but rather a desperate need for narcissistic products. The supply is in forms of many people's worries as well as the emotional hurt of the victim in reaction in response to the triangle.

Through denying, dismissing or justifying the violence, by luring their companions into thinking that it isn't actually happening. This means deflecting any accountability discussions through repetitive discussions and word games so that they are not accountable for their actions.

The victim is subjected to misleading campaigns to denigrate their image and character so that the person who is targeted for violence is left with no source of assistance. This is done by projecting their own violence onto the victim, so that no one believes in their accounts of abuse.

Through the use of a fake charismatic image that makes their victims appear as "bad" ones, they make accusations and then transfer their nastiness attributes onto their friends during their conversations. It's as if they reveal their own strengths and weaknesses to their victims like they were telling them, "Take my disorder here. I'm not interested in this.'

That's exactly what narcissistic violence looks like. And, unfortunately there is no psychology course or diagnosis manual can explain the entire scope of narcissistic aggression, though the methods used to coerce are discovered in several books written by experts in narcissism, reports from mental health professionals who have dealt with victims as clients, and survivors' accounts.

It's the destructive behaviors of a Narcissist and the way they affect us, that is the most important factor to determine whether or not your loved one is a Narcissist. No matter what your age or background it is possible for anyone to become a victim of the narcissistic assault. An abuser who is narcissistic may cause in victims feeling overwhelmed, suicidal or anxious or constantly in a state of flux and utterly useless. If your partner displays certain harmful behaviors

They're at the very least emotionally physically, verbally, and even psychologically violent behaviors. While narcissists who abuse their power are dangerous, relationships with partners who exhibit some of these traits and do not change require an NPD diagnosis in order to motivate victims to recognize that they are dealing with a toxic with their partner.

Chapter 14: The Expressive Handling That You Do Not Recognize

To help you know what the issue is I suggest telling you about a couple I had the pleasure of meeting many years ago. They were the ones I helped through this method of self-awareness and helping. These two people who have two names invented: Robert and Juliet. The case is anonymous. a smart, kind boy who lives a ordinary life. He met a girl, a psychology student. At the time, he was experiencing a period of loneliness. He was a lonely person Things in the world of love didn't work out for him, nor for his job.

This makes people more vulnerable, and they are more likely to become manipulated.

In this girl, he discovered a type of escape as well as unwavering support. However, she experienced an inscrutable emotional manipulation by the girl we'll call her Juliet who was psychologically expertise, such as the ability to manipulate Robert. The manipulations don't always occur with good intentions, however, occasionally a lack of knowledge on the part of a person can withdrawal you to be compelled to manipulate someone else to achieve what you desire. Juliet was suffering from depression, so she threw herself to Robert to help bring her back to life and provide him the affection she was in need of. We can also say Juliet manipulated Robert and helped him to fall in lovewith her, in order to avoid losing him and to be able be sure that someone was always willing to assist her and encourage her.

Robert was a extremely pleasant young man who was a perfectionist, dependable, and servile with a great ability to empathize. All of these qualities were absorbed by Juliet in order she could come out of the depression well in that she had been. As I heard the girl didn't act to harm anyone; he was a excellent person, however, because of depression, was in need of the unwavering help of someone who was not his family. Invisible emotional manipulation has two stages.

The first phase: the catchment

The first thing to do is display your positive side in order that the other person gets a sense of admiration. The process begins with the act of being nice and treating others well as well as giving the best possible, and of doing everything the other person desires.

Who hasn't heard the expression "when we were together was all wonderful and once married is no longer the same".

Some manipulate relationships until they achieve the results they desire, and then they play out an exchange of roles which we'll discuss lateron, as they are confident that the person they want to keep close to them. The manipulator understands what the other person requires and provides it often in excessive amounts to bind a tiny bit to this particular aspect that is so incredibly kind and sensitive. It's a stage in where the manipulator displays all his charisma, is known, and occasionally when he gets the possibility, he puts himself in a more advantageous position than the one being manipulated, offering the victim safety, companionship and unwavering assistance. The goal is earning the respect and trust from the person who is being manipulated.

What did Sandra did to attract Albert? She made her presence known by describing to him the mental work she did in her relationships with acquaintances and friends. She shared with him his work-related activities that she carried out, in order to put himself in a higher level in the realm of mental understanding. She utilized her job to make herself more visible and demonstrate to Albert that he was extremely fortunate to be her a partner and could reach out to her anytime. In the future, the next step was to know more about Albert's mental world, and above all his shortcomings and weaknesses so that she could offer him the help he needed. She was always greeted with flattery and positive feedback, in addition, the communication became regular, every day as well in this way, Albert went through in his life did not have the same weight as the friendship he shared with her.

It is known as invisible emotional manipulation as it isn't noticed, since in the beginning, everything goes well in relationships. The way to recognize it is in the exaggerations. You can be admired by someone and feel affectionate towards your personality, even be envious of you, however, within certain boundaries. When this occurs in over the top, you need to consider what makes them admire your so highly, regardless of whether it's due to a motive of manipulation or the person who is admiring you has poor self-esteem and is comparing you.

In the process of manipulating it is likely that the entire process is likely to have a higher chance of success when the individual also has a particular job, which draws the attention of the person being manipulated and may cause it to change. It is for instance, it is more likely for an overweight person to be in the love of a nutritionist who can help as he admires his profession because he's trying to shed weight. If there's any weakness in the other, then admiration and love will grow. This is the same for someone who is insecure and has a psychologist who can assist her free of charge in friendship, or such as an individual who doesn't have well-being and is not physically fit, surely will be admired by skilled and strong athletes.

When we are feeling that we suffer from a deficit, we look up to those who can fill in what we don't have. If someone is able to excel in a skill which is not present in the other, and then offers assistance for no cost it will speed up the process of becoming in the love of his life because he can put himself in a higher level, that will allow him to gain greater emotional strength.

Second phase: swapping roles

When the manipulator has earned complete trust, love of love and respect for other people He then moves to the next phase of shifting roles. If it was previously an "savior" who gave support and protection to the other person, it now becomes the victim. Because the person you are in the love of her she'll take any action to assist her. Once the love or affection is established then the manipulator takes the control of the situation.

Conclusion

We've come to the final chapter of this book. If I've done my work correctly and you're now aware, you'll be able to have a more clear understanding of who the narcissists and gaslighters have become in the world, as well as how you can take care of them so that you get peace of mind.

I'd like to emphasize that when you're the victim of physical or mental abuse, it is essential to seek out the help of a psychotherapist as soon as you can. The dangers of being victimized emotionally are very real and can be very harmful to your health and well-being. of mind. There have been numerous instances where manipulation and gaslighting strategies have led to individuals suicide. I truly hope to see you succeed and emerge stronger and more successful. One way to ensure you don't end up becoming a victim is to get help!

Support systems a priority as well. Do not hesitate to connect with your family members. Start it right after you finish reading this book. Have a cup of coffee. Reconnect with your friends. Be open to individuals in the world who are concerned for you and would like to see you succeed good. They are often more able to discern, than you do, the areas when your boundaries are being breached. They can give you the confidence you require to free yourself from the narcissist, and to regain your identity and power. People require people. This is the way the world operates. Start by reuniting. Meet new people. Return to the things you enjoy doing. This will be helpful in observing the world in sharp contrast to the nightmare the abuser is trying to get you to accept as reality.

It's a little bit of a difficult task to be a person who is a narcissist in the course of your day, and even be a survivor. It's difficult to accept that they may never change. They're given so many chances, but each time, you are aware of what's to happen. To keep your sanity safe be prepared for the possibility that they'll go back to the lie-teller and cheater, as well as the manipulator they've become. When they're trying to improve, be aware that they'll fall short at times. However, it is important to always make sure you check in to yourself. You need to ensure that you're being a real person in reality and not looking forward to that perfect ending that will never be realized.

After the experience with the narcissist normal to be wondering why you let this occur in the first place. You're wondering what you can do and whether you'll be able to find happiness. You'll probably doubt your self for a moment, and then wallowing in regret, and walking on eggshells , when you don't have to. It's fine. Be gentle and easy with yourself. All that energy you have is directed towards your health, growth and discovering the authentic self that you've lost by trying to become perfect for the perfect narcissist.

After enduring the fire You may feel "done" with love. It could be that you decide you need to get rid of your caring, compassionate self. Do not allow this to occur! Don't let one bad person ruin the goodwill of your heart. You are more than this. Don't let other people's mistakes dictate how you conduct your life. They've already taken much more than they deserve from you. Don't give them any more! Instead, live more confidently and more louder. Bring some of the compassion and empathy towards others toward yourself, and when a self-centered narcissist is in your path You will be determined to avoid any thing that will make you feel less than joyous.

It's a difficult decision to make however, you have to be able to forgive them in order to be able to move on. This isn't meant to mean "forgive but forget." Do not forget, or you'll end in in the same spot and again! Be kind to forgive however, be mindful to remember. Remember to ensure that you don't allow them in again, unless at your own discretion. Keep in mind how they hurt you so that you don't have to repeat it. Recalling your past can make you feel powerful, since it's in your right to take revenge, but you're above the fact that you've decided to forget and forgive.

Live, love and live unconditionallyand take your mind along on the journey. Experiments are excellent instructors. You've attended a class in Narcissist 101. There's no reason to go through it again. If there's a thing you should be grateful for, it's the fact that once you've finally found the person you are, when you are finally free of the narcissist in you, you'll grow stronger and better because of it. You'll be able help others in the same way as you, who are seeking help, beg to be noticed. I'm talking about people who hope that someone just like you is able to find a match that can spark a flame in their souls, to the point that, similar to you a fiery flame can start to burn inside them in such a way that they find the courage to break free.

For the narcissist, don't hold hatred in the pit of your soul. Send them all the best. Make yourself feel the same way. And then get to the task of discovering who you are.

www.ingramcontent.com/pod-product-compliance
Lightning Source LLC
Chambersburg PA
CBHW060328030426
42336CB00011B/1250